Faith and Conflict

Reflections on Christian Faiths' Impact on the Rise of the Holocaust

Eugen Schoenfeld

Copyright © 2011 Eugen Schoenfeld Ph.D
All rights reserved.

ISBN: 1456522051
ISBN-13: 9781456522056

Acknowledgement

"Gene!" I turned around to confront the caller. It was a sunny morning in the neighborhood tennis club and Kay was right behind me. "Hey," she said "I just wanted to tell you that Bob and I just returned from visiting the Holy Land." She was aware of my Holocaust experience and felt that I would be interested in her experiences in the Holy Land – which I was. "Did you enjoy your trip?" I inquired. "It was marvelous." Kay was totally committed to the Catholic Church, and as she related to us her trip which to was indeed an emotional experience. There was, however, one curious aspect in her description of her trip. She continually referred to the country she visited as the Holy Land and never mentioned the State of Israel. Finally I could not contain myself. "Kay" I said "indeed the land is Holy but the country that encompass the Holy Land is the State of Israel." Her response was angry and vehement: "No! She declared with a heightened voice. "It is and will always be the Holy Land."

I could not understand her anger and her denial of Israel. She never acted with hostility to me or to any other Jew in the club. This must have been something else. This seemed like Kay's denial of State of Israel's legitimacy. I was confronted with the question what motivated her to deny Israel's legitimacy and defend the idea of the Holy Land?

Kay's refusal to acknowledge the legitimacy Israel as an independent state, I realized, was not her unique and a personal perspective. Most likely, as an extremely devout Catholic Kate's response the

Vatican's point of view. the Vatican did not acknowledge Israel as a state till 1992, forty four years after its de facto existence and even then the Vatican did not desire to exchange ambassadors with Israel as it did with other countries. Why?

The Vatican has advanced a number of reasons for not accepting Israel as a legitimate State. Among the reasons Vatican cited was its fear for the fate of the Catholics residing in Israel and other Muslim countries. All their excuses are, in my view, (and it may be a cynical view), attempts to disguise the real historical Catholic perspective which from the time of the Crusades, advocated a belief, if not openly but surely sub-rosa, that the land which is now called Israel belongs to historical Catholicism as their Holy Land the birth place of Jesus.

It is this episode and others of similar content that led to speculate regarding Christianity's negation of Judaism's and its legitimacy. I began speculative explorations. Speculative explorations are difficult because one can easily become tied up to one's own biases. I wanted to share my early ideas with some persons whose views and knowledge I respect. The two persons who after reading my initial essays encouraged me to continue with my speculative essays were my cousin Dr. Gustav Schonfeld and Mel Hecker.

Gus and I share a common history. We both were born in Munkacs in a Carpathian shtetl, we had similar early education, both of us survived the same concentration camps and both have immigrated to the United States. Gus achieved success in medicine and retired as the Chair of Medicine at Washington University where he held many endowed chairs and yet continued his interest on the causes of the Holocaust. Gus believed in my views and encouraged me to make them public. Mr. Mel Hecker is the editor of a monumental work – The United States Holocaust Memorial Museum Encyclopedia of Camps and Ghettos 1933-1945. I have a tendency not to express fully my thoughts as though I expect others to innately understand my ideas. Moreover, I tend to meander and stray from scholarly discipline. Mel brings me back to reality and shows me the occasional convalutedness of my thinking and with his help I find the right intellectual direction. For all your help in keeping me on the straight path I am very grateful.

I am also extremely grateful to Sandra Cutler who edited my manuscript. This is a thankless job often very tedious. She did it with grace and proficiency. Sandra is involved with the Atlanta Jewish community and she too encouraged me to write my observations that I present in the essays collected in this book.

I am also grateful to Michael Berenbaum for writing the preface to my book. Michael is one of the foremost and world-wide known Holocaust scholars. His addition to my work endows mine with the gravitas that only a great scholar can do. Thank you also for your encouragement.

Of course I could have not completed this work without my wife's encouragement. Jean stood by me for sixty-one years in good times and bad ones and always encouraged my intellectual endeavors. She counteracted my propensity for laziness. Indeed she is the epitome of woman of valor whose husband and children call blessed.

25th of Teveth 5771
January 1, 2011

Faith and Conflict

Reflections on Christian Faiths' Impact on the Rise of the Holocaust

Eugen Schoenfeld

Table of Contents

Preface xx
Foreword xi
Prologue xx
I   Introduction 1
        The Roots of My Perspective: 1
II   Perspectives on the Holocaust 27
        God and the Holocaust 29
        The Causes of Holocaust: A Sociological Perspective 47
III   Christian-Jewish Dialectic 73
        Isaac and Jesus 75
        Love and Justice: The Bifurcation of Jewish Christian Values ... 99
        Justice: An Elusive Concept in Christianity 111
IV   Solutions to Inter-Ethnic and Inter-Religious Hostilities .. 131
        The inadequacy of Tolerance 133
        Moral Universalism 149
        Abraham and Moral Universalism xxx
V   Epilogue 171
        Zachor: Remembering the Holocaust 171

Foreword

Michael Berenbaum

Several times a year I am asked to write a foreword or an epilogue to a survivor's memoir and whenever possible I agree for it is a privilege to assist in bringing their story to the public and if my name and the few words I have to offer enables the story to come forward, how can I say no!

Eugen Schoenfeld has written a work that is neither a memoir nor a work of scholarship. It is a hybrid, part one and part the other. His story is told in fragments. He is not writing for a scholarly audience, but using the tools of his profession and the insights of his life – insights that come from painful and very difficult experience – to offer the truths that he has discovered during the four score and five years that he has graced this earth. If not now, then when. And at his age, at his stage in life, there is no reason not to be forthcoming, not to speak with the might of his wisdom and the pain of his insight.

My introduction will also be a hybrid, filling in some of the missing historical information but more important engaging with some of the issues that Eugen Schoenfeld has raised. I take my clue from the Talmudic injunction that in a dispute for the sake of heaven, both sides will be sustained.

A word of our time: I write these words on the eve of Yom Kippur, Judaism's most sacred day. The Day of Judgment is the formal name for Yom Kippur even though the translation of Yom Kippur is Day of Atonement. We both have difficulties not with God as judge but with holding God responsible for evil in the world. We both agree that we humans are responsible for the evil in a world. It is our creation and our responsibility to rectify.

I write these words also in the midst of the anger that is reflected n contemporary America, the anger over an Islamic Cultural Center in Lower Manhattan and the anger of the Tea Party, the anger at undocumented immigrants – illegal aliens – the anger at President Obama and at our political class.

We are also in the last years of survivors. Schoenfeld who was but a child when the war began, the year of his Bar Mitzvah is now in his mid eighties. The perpetrators have departed the world. The Angel of Death arrived before the bar of justice and their victims are aging.

Schoenfeld says in passing that he was born in Munkacs in the Sub-Carpathia. Born in Czechoslovakia, he was deported from a town that was incorporated into Hungary as incentive for Hungary joining German as an ally. The town was unique, as was the region. Fervently Orthodox and notoriously anti-Zionist, his family was unusual in the modernity of their Orthodoxy and also because they could embrace a transformation of the Jewish people that came at the initiation of human beings rather than the Divine. The objection to Zionism was not the goal, the restoration of the Jewish people to their land, but the means. Such a restoration was to be the work of the Messiah, God's initiative and not humanity's. Schoenfeld has embraced his father's values even as he understood them in their sociological context. His childhood world was totally Jewish; he was aware of other, but it was they who were strange not he. They were the "other." He never saw himself as that.

Anti-Semitism was an external threat and precautions were taken. Jews did not leave their house at Easter, when Christians remembered the crucifixion and when Matthew account blaming the Jews and their descendents were read and the chant was heard regarding "perfidious Jews." Easter was about hope to the Christians, salvation. To the Jews of his town, it was a time of fear. We hear echoes of distrust of Christianity throughout his work. Their response was to hunker down: forbearance and fortitude. Schoenfeld's is more challenging, more engaging.

We agree that evil does not come from God but from us. The absence of justice in our world is our responsibility to change. Most painful is the evil inflicted by humanity in the name of God, pretending that it is the Divine will and not human choice. He rejects the notion that evil as a test from God or punishment form God and also that we cannot understand the Divine, three tried and true ways of defending God and alleviating responsibility for evil in the world.

We disagree about a question he once asked his father: How could such evil happen in the 20th Century? The expectation is wrong. The 20th century is not a century of moral progress but of technological progress often at the expense of morality. My teacher Richard Rubenstein who also approached the Holocaust sociologically argued in The Cunning of History that the Holocaust was an expression in the extreme of what is common to the mainstream of Western Civilization. The Holocaust could have only occurred in the 20th century with its technological advancement and bureaucratic mechanisms of control. Rubestein wrote: Perhaps the spirit of the 20th century was seldom expressed as well as by Maxim Gorky in his tale of the peasant who confessed that he had killed another peasant and stolen his cow during the Russian Revolution. The murder was worried that he might be prosecuted for theft. When asked whether was afraid he might also be prosecuted for murder, the peasant replied: "That is nothing: people now come cheaply."

Schoenfeld displays the tenacity of his father and the piety of his ancestors when he grapples with the struggle between Justice and

Mercy. He reaffirms what he considers Judaism's ongoing belief in human perfectibility. I suspect that we both come closer to concurring that Judaism believes not that humanity can become perfect but less imperfect. We do not have to be tomorrow what we were yesterday.

His writings on anomie and the destruction of social predictability and the fear and the chaos that such condition bring have much to say to 21st century America and not just mid 1930s Germany. The yearning for the mythological status quo ante was great in both societies. The stranger becomes the threat, the cause of all problems. But Schoenfeld caution, "these strangers are no wanderers, they are people who came and stayed."

Every survivor is asked: "Can it happen here?" Schoenfeld answers affirmatively, but without a very important caveat, "Not if we remain true to American values and Constitutional guarantees, separation of powers, checks and balances, inalienable rights, restraint on the power of government.

Schoenfeld feels no need to be polite and portrays Judaism and Christianity as rivals, as emphasizing different values and different responsibilities. He sees the tension between them focused on the issue of justice and mercy. Judaism, he proudly proclaims insists on Justice, justice tempered by mercy, but not mercy without justice. There are duties that must be performed, deeds that must be done. He contrast Isaac and Jesus and is precise in his depiction of how and why the Jesus narrative reshaped the Isaac story and removed some pivotal elements form it. He views supercessionism as part of Christianity from its inception and is suspicion of salvation by grace: salvation must be hard won. Far worse than the absence of grace is cheap grace and the false sense of confidence – arrogance that it inspires.

His critique of Christianity is deep. He asks: Has the absence of accountability in Christianity contributed to the historic hostility toward Jews? Does the primacy of love distract from the social system's requirement for justice? Does it result in an insistence on charity, agape rather than an ethics of justice which seeks to rectify the social system and not just aid the individual? These are important question.

We part company on his estimation of the post-war penance of the Church. You will read his view, so permit me to tell you mine.

It is a paradox of the Holocaust that the innocent feel guilty and the guilty innocent. The two most innocent Pope, those who sided with the Jews and assisted them – Pope John XXIII and John Paul II – did the most of eliminate some significant causes of anti-Semitism within the Church. They did much, not as much as he or I would have liked, but still very much, often without quite saying how much they were doing or why it was so necessary to change the culture of the Church. The results have been far from perfect but they have ushered in the most important and peaceful period in Catholic-Jewish relations. We will yearn for these times in the future.

We do not part company on his critique of tolerance. I will let you read his critique. May I only add the most important critique of tolerance at the very formation of the American political experience? George Washington wrote to the Newport Hebrew Congregation in 1791: "It is now no more that toleration is spoken of as if it were the indulgence of one class of people that another enjoyed the exercise of their inherent natural rights, for, happily, the Government of the United States, which gives to bigotry no sanction, to persecution no assistance, requires only that they who live under its protection should demean themselves as good citizens in giving it on all occasions their effectual support."

Tolerance presumes that one side dominates and grants what does not rightfully belong to the other. We must embrace and celebrate diversity in our world and has standard of action, "requires only that they who live under its protection should demean themselves as good citizens in giving it on all occasions their effectual support.

Finally, we join hands in understanding the survivor's response to the Holocaust. Consciousness of the Holocaust has moved way beyond the Jewish community.

In the past sixty five years the bereaved memories of a parochial community have been transformed into an act of conscience. Survivors have responded in the most deeply Jewish way of all: remembering suffering and transmitting that memory in order to fortify conscience, to plead for decency, to strengthen values and thus to intensify a commitment to human dignity. That is how the Biblical Jews taught us to remember that we were slaves in Egypt and that is why the Biblical experience has framed the struggle for freedom ever since.

One cannot undo what has happened. Historians can answer the question how; theologians, writers, poets and philosopher have not answered the question why. Yet we can answer the question of what to do with this history. Embrace it, study it, wrestle with it and ultimately transform it into a weapon for the human spirit to enlarge our sense of responsibility, to alleviate human suffering and strengthen our moral resolve.

For Eugen Schoenfeld as for many survivors, bearing witness conferred a sense of meaning in the aftermath of atrocity. They have told the story of the past, to keep a promise they made to those they left behind. More importantly, they have told the story of the past in the hope that it can transform the future.

Section One

The Roots of my Perspective

I, like most children, grew up in a sheltered world. My world was the Jewish community of Munkacs in Sub Carpathia. For approximately eight hundred years before the Treaty of Versailles marking the end of World War I the city of my birth was part of Hungary. But with the political reconstruction of Europe in 1918 it became a part of a new country: Czechoslovakia. Munkacs was a shtetl not only because the majority of its population was Jewish but also, and perhaps primarily because, it exuded a Jewish ambiance. When the steam whistle of the communal bath-house blew Friday evening announcing the arrival of the Sabbath – all business in the city stopped. Jews in their Chassidic garb hurried out of their homes to the synagogues and the spirit of the Sabbath – a world sans mercantilism decedent on the city. I lived on a street in which all of the thirty some families who dwelled there, with the exception of one, were Jewish. One could say that the Jewish families living in St. Martin Street formed a "gemeinschaft", a village community in which each family knew and was in contact with all the others on the street. As a child I was welcomed into all the Jewish homes and frequently I have chosen to have my Sabbath meal with one of the neighbors because, as I informed my mother, their "cholent"

Faith and Conflict

(a bean and barley casserole usually served on the Sabbath) was better than hers. Even as a young child of five I freely, uninvited and unannounced entered the homes of any of our neighbors and was given a seat at their table.

Though anti-Semitism during my childhood existed in the city I knew nothing of it. I was aware that there were people who were different from us. For instance, I became conscious that Anna, our maid who spoke Yiddish and who made sure that I recited my morning prayers, was different. Still, I could not understand, for instance, why on certain days, which I later I became aware were Easter and Christmas, she went some place other than a synagogue to pray.

I must have been about six years old when I first became conscious of the existence of Christians as a separate entity. I distinctly remember that day. It was a late November afternoon when I was going home from visiting the Kalus family I heard loud squealing coming from the courtyard of the non-Jewish neighbor whom I never visited. The noise intrigued me and therefore I decided to be brave and enter the courtyard and investigate the commotion. The gate to the courtyard was unlocked. I pushed the gate and entered. In the courtyard I encountered a scene that I have never experienced. There on a sturdy limb of a tree a live pig was hung by its feet oozing blood oozing from its neck into a pail that was constantly stirred by a woman. The pig was alive squealing loudly and no one there was bothered by it. Next to the pig was a large bonfire. The sound of the pig together with the fire next to it made it an eerie scene. I hurriedly left the courtyard but the memory of the pig being slaughtered has remained as a horrifying experience. Indeed, these people were quite different from the others who lived in the street.

Slowly I became aware that there were many people who were different from us. People who ate different foods, dressed and talked differently from us. I did not judge them as being either superior or inferior to us except that I felt strangely among them for they were not like me and I did not feel at ease in the same manner as I did in the homes of my Jewish neighbors. I was curious about these different people without being judgmental.

The market place just around the corner from my street on Mondays and Thursdays was filled with people who dressed and spoke quite differently from us. They sat on the cobble stoned floor selling their chickens, eggs, sunflower seeds and corn flower. I often accompanied my mother to the market square listening to her conversations in another language and watching her bargaining in the process of buying their commodities. The process of bargaining was conducted in a hostile tone. It was almost verbal confrontation that ended with either an exchange of money or parting with sardonic comments. This was when I realized that the women and the men dressed in the rough wool and flax garments were treated as inferiors by my mother. When I asked why I was simply told – they are peasants.

My first awareness that there were others who were not only different from us but that they were also hostile to us and therefore I should avoid them or at least be very careful in my interaction with them was when I was about seven or eight years old.

Every spring at the beginning of Passover my grandmother took me to her home about thirty five miles from Munkacs to Talamas a small village on the crest of the Carpathian Mountains. I spent the eight days of Passover holiday with them so that they should not be alone for the Seder a ritual performed on the eve of Passover. Of course I was there so that I should recite the traditional four questions that Jewish children ask their parents. During one stay when Easter Sunday and Passover coincided, my grandmother asked me not to leave the house on Easter Sunday. I was greatly disappointed because I was asked to forgo playing with my friends. "Why should I stay in the house?" I asked. "I am afraid that the young peasant boys will try to hurt you" grandmother answered. "Why would they do that?" I continued to query her. "Because on this day" she stated very sadly" the Christians

Faith and Conflict

are being taught by their priests that we Jews have killed their god and they are angry at us." This was my introduction to anti-Semitism.

By the age of ten I began my studies of the history of Jews. I began with the help of my tutor to read Simon Dubnow's History of the Jews in Hebrew. I became familiar with the Jewish tragedies including those experienced by Jews during the Crusades, the Spanish Inquisition, the Dreyfuss Affair and many more. Still, these were lessons in history and anti-Semitism did not have the personal impact on me as did my personal experiences in the Holocaust.

With time my experiences with anti-Semitism became more frequent, more intense and more complex and above all personal. In early November 1938 at the Vienna conference between Adolph Hitler, Benito Mussolini, Neville Chamberlain (Prime Minister of England) and Edourd Daladier (Prime Minister of France) Munkacs my hone in the Sub-Carpathian region was transferred from Czechoslovakia to Hungary. This agreement was championed by Chamberlain as an attempt to appease Hitler hoping to avert what a year later was to become World War II.

The change of government not only meant that I had to learn a relatively new language but also that the Hungarians taking over the city introduced anti-Semitic laws that were already instituted by that government in the early 1930s. For the next five years, under the Hungarian regime life for Jews in Munkacs became more difficult and it culminated with the greatest of all anti-Semitic acts – the Holocaust.

All these experiences have led me to ask even in my teens: Why are the Christians hostile to us Jews? Let me be emphatic: The anti-Semitism that I experienced during the Holocaust although seemingly secular has its origins and its roots in the Christian religion. It began with the anti-Semitic laws instituted by Constantine the Great and continued ever since. Having been a dispersed minority in the Christian world, Jews never dared to challenge, at least publicly, the legitimacy of the hostile laws and acts under which they lived. I was taught not to challenge Christians. I was also taught to become invisible. It was strongly impressed on me that I must withdraw from the public world hoping that humility and submissiveness will reduce anti-Jewish hostility. Above all, I was taught not to rock the boat and not give the Christians cause to become violent against us.

I must admit that some events that Jews consider to be a part of the "Jewish Tragedies" like the destruction of both Temples, the Macabbean Wars against Greece were not anti-Semitic acts, they were political events. They were merely the consequences of the Babylonian, the Syrian, the Greek, and Roman empire building. Modern anti-Semitism is different. It is the consequence the introduction of hostilities against Jews and their religion. It began when Christianity assumed a dialectical perspective, when they became the anti-thesis to the Jewish thesis. It has arisen in the process of Christianity's desire to supersede the legitimacy of Jews as the bearers of the true religion. This perspective was the consequence of the First Council of Nicaea (325 C.E.) Christian anti-Semitism and led to Constantine's anti-Jewish laws as well as to the anti-Semitic teaching of St. Chrysostom. From the time of Constantine all Jewish tragedies were the result of anti-Semitism rooted in the Christian theological perspectives. These tragedies arose out of the Christian perspective of Jews and led, for example, the Crusaders massacre of Jews, the massacres in York England, the expulsion of Jews from France by Louis the Ninth, the Inquisitions in Spain and Portugal, the restriction imposed on Jews to live in ghettos, the massacres in Russia known as the pogroms and the various laws expelling Jews from legitimate occupations. Of course the greatest of all tragedies was the Holocaust in which most of my family was massacred in Auschwitz.

My personal experiences with this last Jewish tragedy began in November 1938 when I turned thirteen. As soon as the Hungarians took over the Czech territories which included my home town the Jews in those areas began to experience the consequences anti-Jewish

Faith and Conflict

laws that were already in force in pre 1938 Hungary. For instance, I soon learned what was meant by <u>numerus clasus</u>. This Latin term was a euphemism for a legal quota system that decreed that only seven percent of businesses in the city could be owned by Jews. In a town where almost two-thirds of the city's population of 27,000 was Jewish, this decree meant that most Jews lost their businesses licenses and their livelihood. Hungarian anti-Jewish laws later on, especially with regards to university attendance advocated <u>numerus nullus</u> namely the prohibition to admit Jews to colleges and universities. Jewish students in the Gymnasiums, the high-schools, found that their path for a professional future that required university training had been curtailed. Life of freedom and equality as we experienced during the Czech regime came to a halt. Still we managed to exist and live in our homes. We have hoped when the war that began in 1939 and especially after the United States joined the fight will soon end with the Allies victory and we will be able to resume living a peaceful, normal, and predictable life. Meanwhile, the prevailing Jewish philosophy was to "hunker-down", to become invisible, and above all else not rock the boat. We believed, as Jews did for almost two millennia, that in time of anti-Jewish hostilities will end and meanwhile we needed to be patient, to be silent, and the calamity will pass.

When the World War II started, Hungary, as expected, became a German ally. There was a general mobilization and all Christian young men were subscripted into the army. Jews could not be trusted, was the official point of view, so instead of the army they were placed into labor camps or as the Hungarians called it "work-service" which was considered to be an extension of the army. Wearing army caps with civvies with a yellow arm band, instead of guns Jews were issued shovels and pick axes. When the war between Germany and Russia broke out, the Jewish young men in the work service were taken to the front lines where they were assigned to dig fox-holes and clear the mines from captured Russian soil.

The Roots of my Perspective

My Holocaust experience led me to raise an important question about the world in which we Jews lived. The best way I can describe how the Holocaust experience affected my thinking is to share with you an episode that occurred on my first day in the concentration camp Auschwitz II-also called Birkenau.

After we disembarked from the train that brought us to Auschwitz, and after having passed muster before Dr. Mengele, we were deprived of our clothes, shorn, deloused, and sent to the showers. We were issued our inmate blue and gray striped cotton uniforms with our numbers (mine was 90138) and a yellow triangle sewn on the left breast side of the jacket. We were told that the only item that we brought from home that we could keep were our shoes. As I entered the large room filled with shower heads, I was given a small bar of soap and was told to proceed to take a shower. I took of my shoes and placed them together with the others in the corner of the room. After the shower I proceeded to retrieve my shoes that because of my deformed arches were fitted to my feet. I was one of the last to seek my shoes and found that someone inadvertently took one of my shoes and I was left with two right shoes. I tried to rectify the mistake but, no one responded to my request for exchanging the wrong shoe. I explained my problem to one of the roaming Kapos (inmate supervisors) and sought his advice. He pointed to a window behind which was a small room. "Knock on the window" the Kapo instructed me "and when it opens up tell those inside what has happened. Perhaps they may give you a pair of wooden soled shoes. However," he continued, "you must begin your request by saying in German: Ich bitte gehorsham (I am humbly requesting) and then proceed to tell them your problem." A pair of wooden soled shoes is better than none, I thought to myself, and proceeded to the window. I knocked on the window and it opened. Behind it there were two persons – a German SS with his rifle and an inmate wearing an armband with "Kapo" printed on it. Before I could speak, the Kapo hit me on my head with a heavy wooden stick that would have made an

Faith and Conflict

admirable Irish shillelagh, after which he asked me in German" what do you want?" Based on the advice given me and speaking in German I began with "Ich bitte gehorsham" and continued to ask for a pair of shoes. The Kapo wasn't interested in my request. Perhaps he sought to demonstrate to the SS his inhumanity in a place where such traits were rewarded. He took his gnarled stick hit me over the head again and closed the window. I returned to my father crying. "I am not crying" I told him "because the beating hurt me." Of course it did. I was crying I told my father because of frustration and disillusionment with humanity. "How can it be" I asked my father "that today in the middle of the twentieth century in spite of advancement, in the sciences and philosophy human beings still retain their pre-human bestial character? The question that I asked my father then still haunts me today. The inhumanity that I experienced in the concentration camps continues to exist even today and hence the question I asked my father then is still also valid today. The questions for which I seek explanations consist of the following: What is the reason behind the rise of the Holocaust. Why have Jews been singled out for destruction? And, finally, how can we eliminate the conditions that have led to anti-Semitism for almost two millennia.

My Weltanschauung:

My world view is not the product of my Holocaust experiences alone. The way I see the world, the content of my philosophy of life, my moral ideals that I believe should govern human relationships have been influenced by Jewish theology, by Jewish history, by sociology my profession and above all by my father's political and philosophical perspectives. So that the reader may understand my point of view exemplified in the essays in this book, I need to review my life in Munkacs a small town in the Carpathian region and the various experiences that have influenced my perspective of life.

I was born into a family strictly adhering to Torah laws. I grew up in Munkacs in Hungarian or Mukacevo as it was called when it became a part of the Czechoslovakian Republic. About two-thirds of the city's population was Jewish and most of them were Orthodox. From my father, who at that time was a modern Orthodox Jew, I inherited a commitment to the importance of scholarliness and rationality. From my maternal grandfather who was a Chassidic Jew who wore the traditional silk caftan (bekeshe) with a fur hat (shtramel) on Shabbath and was a follower of Vizsnitzer rebbe, I inherited the belief in a loving universal God and the importance of loving humanity. He taught me to love mercy and to seek a personal relationship with God. To me, following my maternal grandfather's beliefs, God was an approachable entity. He could be questioned and he could even be accused of injustice. I was told stories in which God was even forced to defend Himself

Faith and Conflict

in a Beth-Din a rabbinical court having been accused of violating his own laws of justice. From my teachers, my parents and grandparents I have gained the view that the single and most significant ideal is justice. Justice is the sine qua non of all morals without which the human world cannot exist. Jewish legends, that were part of my education, tell us that there are always thirty-six just and righteous persons walking the earth on whose account God will never destroy the world as He did with Sodom and Gomorrah.

From my paternal grandfather and my father I inherited a commitment to Talmudic Judaism which stresses the importance of a universal moral law. From my maternal grandfather I inherited the belief that above all else one must be an "eidler" man a sensitive and an empathetic person. Both grandparents considered Judaism to be a faith and were committed to the strict adherence to the Mosaic and Talmudic commandments. Both followed the rigorous and strictly defined path that is known as the Halachah. Both of them were guided by the teachings enunciated in the Shulchan Aruch, a book written by Joseph Caro (1488-1575) in which the author codified Jewish laws and customs. Both placed primacy on faith in God and observance of mitzvoth (commandments) and accepted the dogmatism of ritual. Both accepted the idea of unquestioned adherence and neither of them was concerned with Jewish history. Both the Talmudic and Chassidic oriented Jews have for two thousand years placed centrality to the belief of national redemption is associated with the coming of the Messiah when God in His mercy will redeem the Jews from the Diaspora and return them to the Land of Israel. However, by the twentieth century Judaism was no longer a homogeneous belief system. Orthodoxy was giving way to heterodoxy to diversity in Jewish belief.

In the eighteenth century, Orthodox Judaism in Europe became bifurcated. On the one hand there were those who believed that the observance of the commandments and Talmudic learning as the absolute requirement for personal salvation. They literally accepted

My Weltanschauung:

the Torah command that decrees that it is every Jews' duty to study the Torah, both the written and the oral Torah day and night. (The written Torah consists of the Bible especially the first five books and the oral Torah is the Talmud.)

On the other hand there were those who were members of the new sect started by Baal Shem Tov (The Master of the Great Name) the founder of Chassidism whose beliefs and views differed from the earlier rabbis" Like their master the Baal Shem his disciples known as "rebbes" became the charismatic leaders of this rapidly expanding movement. The Chassidim, the followers of the charismatic rebbes came from the lower economic and less educated classes – the lower socio-economic strata. In contrast to learning, Chassidic Jews stressed the primacy joyful relationship between man and God. They stressed the idea of "hitlahavuth" the need for the experiential dimension of religion – that is to put one's soul on fire.

Family Influences:

I was influenced by both my paternal and maternal grandfathers. My father following his father's views gave primacy to knowledge and study. His greatest joy would have been if I were to become a Talmudic scholar and be identified in the community as a "harif" one who possess a keen and sharp mind. Yet, at the same time he was also a modernist. He didn't believe in the ritualized rigid Yeshivah, the traditional rabbinic education, instead he hired a learned rabbi who was less dogmatic than Yeshivah rabbis with whom I studied every afternoon for four hours five days a week till I was eighteen.

My maternal grandfather, on the other hand, living in a small village in the midst of the Carpathian Mountains was, as indicated earlier,

Faith and Conflict

was a Chassid, a follower of the famous Vizsnitzer Rebbe. From him I learned the importance of the quality of human relationship. The Chassidism placed primacy not on learning but on the joy of life and the love of God who was to be found in nature. For instance, the famous Chassidic rabbi of Berdichev, Levi Yitzchak often communed with and prayed to God in the meadows and the forests surrounding his town.

In such an atmosphere Levi Yitzchak developed a personal relationship with God. It was there that Levi Yitzchak not only spoke with God but also argued with him and even accused Him of acting unjustly toward the Jews. My grandfather Avrohom sought to emulate his rabbi's qualities and become an eidler man – a sensitive and caring individual.

The fundamental human relationship advocated by the Chassidim is based on the love of God, love of nature and love of their fellow human beings. Their fervent desire was to attain a spiritual communion with God. It is this philosophy that influenced the great scholar Martin Buber and it has also influenced me. Instead of Talmud, my grandfather Avrohom was punctilious to recite each day a portion of psalms – the "t'hilim." This did not mean that the Chassidim opposed Talmudic scholarship. To the contrary! They admired learned people and wished that their rebbe would be a scholar so that they could take pride in him as a harif, an intellectually sharp person. But when learning was not possible, as for instance among the working people, the joyful love of God and his people was more than sufficient for gaining salvation. They fervently believed that love and joy, and of course, the observance of the laws would make a person meritorious in the eyes of God and will gain a portion in the world to come. I remember when my maternal-grandfather on the way to the synagogue on one Sabbath pointed to another Jew also on his way to services. "Tuli," he said "you see that man he is truly an eidler mensch." This was the greatest compliment he could bestow on that person. It is not because he was a learned person, not a person with a sharp mind, but my grandfather singled him out because he was a sensitive and caring person.

In a sense these divergent Orthodox Jewish groups represented two different perspectives of God. On the one hand the Talmudic scholars reflect the intellectual essence of God, the Torah's legalism, and the concern with principles of democracy founded on justice. The Chassidic perspective was rooted in Jewish mysticism in the Kabala that placed primacy on God's empathetic side of rechem – mercy. (It is interesting that the Hebrew word rechem i.e., mercy also connotes the female womb in a sense indicating God's male orientation resides in justice and his female nature is expressed by his mercy.)

In short, these two Jewish religious philosophies imparted to me a scholar's concern for justice and the humanitarian concern for love and mercy. For these two qualities are but the two sides of the same coin. There is a Talmudic tale that tells us that when God decided to create the human world he consulted with his angels. He asked them "should I create the world that will be solely governed by the principle of justice or, shall I create it and endow the world with the principle of mercy?" Answering his hypothetical question, God mused: "If I were to create the world based on justice alone, who could withstand the purity and harshness of the principle of justice but, should I to create the world on mercy alone then there would be no order and law." Therefore God first created the world the principle of justice which then He mitigated it by mercy. (See Bialik and Ravnitzky) In sum my Judaism is the product of Jewish learning and Chassidic spiritualism.

Faith and Conflict

Zionism: A New Spiritual movement

My father also instilled in me a commitment to Zionism into this new perspective Jewish perspective that advocated the need to establish a Jewish State – the State of Israel. He was a Zionist and one of the founders of the secular Hebrew school in my city in which the language of instruction was Modern Hebrew. He believed in the adage coined by Eliezer ben Yehudah that the revival of the Jewish nation must co-exist with the revival of its language.

Zionism the new Jewish secular and nationalist movement arose at the fin des sciecle and provided me with a new perspective that served as an additional root for my Jewish identity. The term Zionism was coined in 1886 by Nathan Birnbaum describing the movement that placed primacy on the ancient Jewish belief of returning to Zion.* Zionism introduced an emphasis on secular, moral, philosophical, and historical dimensions of being Jewish. Unlike religion that was a-political and stressed ritual observances, Zionism was rooted in a political belief that stressed the re-creation of Israel as a modern nation. Zionism rejected the self deprecatory notion that Jews lost their homeland because of their sins. The rise of Zionism was influenced by the Jewish enlightenment (Haskalah) and it was also a response to the Dreyfus affair.

The Jewish enlightenment was a quasi secular movement that began in Germany towards the end of the 18th century and sought to replace the medieval Jewish religion mired in mysticism and superstition with "sehel" (sense and rationality). But the idea of nationalism, that is, the advocacy to returning to their ancient land where Jews could assume their rightful place among nations was a reaction to millennia of Jewish persecution. The latest of such persecutions occurred in France which was the mother of modern ideals of liberty, equality,

Zionism: A New Spiritual movement

and brotherhood. Jews soon realized that these morals slogans advocated in France did not include Jews, just like the U.S. constitution's guaranty of freedom did not include the black slaves. The event that led Jews to realize that the powerful ideals of the French revolution excluded Jews was the Dreyfus incident. The Dreyfus affair occurred at the end of the nineteenth century. Alfred Dreyfus a captain in the French Army was accused and was found guilty of treason. His accusers, primarily the army and the Church, based their accusations on falsified evidence that indicted him of having sold military secrets to the Germans and Italians. The heads of the French Army knowing that the indictment was based on documents forged by the perpetrator Colonel Eszterhazy and his collaborators especially Colonel Henry, did none the less in a secret trial convict Captain Dreyfus and sent him to Devil's Island. Dreyfus the Jew became the escape-goat for Eszterhazy who was of Christian and of Hungarian nobility. However, through the efforts of many including Alfred's brother Mathieu and Emile Zola, the noted French author, the truth came out. The French Government acquiescing to the army and with the support of the Jesuits refused to grant a re-trial. But the case became a cause célèbre brought so much notoriety and turmoil in France that in August 1899 Dreyfus was brought back to France from his prison in "Devil's Island. " He was re-tried and found innocent and subsequently was reinstated into the Army.

This episode coupled with the long history of Christian atrocities against Jews led many Jews, including my father, to believe that Jews would never experience security and be safe from anti-Semitism and persecution until they would be able to reside in their own land. Such experiences and associated views gave birth to Zionism that became an alternative foundation to Jewish identity. Orthodox Jews rejected Zionism and their attempt to re-establish Israel as a Jewish State. They considered such an act blasphemous because they firmly believed that liberation from anti-Semitism and the establishment of Israel would only occur at the time of the coming of the Messiah and

Faith and Conflict

that time will be ordained by God. No one, Orthodox Jews argued, has the right to usurp God's prerogatives. The time, the place, and the mode for the liberation of Jews will be determined only by God who through his mercy will liberate the Jews from the yoke of Christians and Muslims. Just as He delivered the Jews from Egypt so will He deliver the Jews through the Messiah from Christian oppression. It is only then and through the Messiah's efforts that Jews will re-establish the Holy Temple in Jerusalem and re-introduce the ancient sacrificial rituals and Israel will become again the theocracy like it was in the past.

In my youth my brother, sister, and I, arising early on the Sabbath joined our parents in their bed. It is there that my father talked to me about world events and about socialism as a political orientation. For him Israel, following the teachings of Theodor Herzl outlined in his book "Alt Neu Land" must become the model for modern societies and it must reflect human social concerns. Through my Saturday conversations with him I became acquainted with St. Simon and above all else with the views of Anatole France. Although my father perceived himself a socialist, he was not a socialist as the term is used today. Unfortunately, the term socialism because of ignorance and political expediency has been given a negative connotation. Although his political perspective was left of center my father's orientation is best described as a humanitarian and as an entrepreneur – an owner of a book store. While he was decidedly committed to free enterprise it did not diminish his concern for the well being of humanity. I must say that I inherited this propensity. It seems that these Sabbath talks primed me to become concerned with social issues, with human issues, and with human welfare and influenced me to become a sociologist.

In addition to the influence of Chassidism and Zionism I was and still am greatly influenced by my studies of Jewish history. History taught me that Christian belief was and continues to be anti-Jewish.

Zionism: A New Spiritual movement

Although rooted in Judaism, Christianity sought to acquire its own identity and to do so Christianity had to become the anti-thesis to the Jewish thesis. In my essays included in this book I examine the Christian belief system and point out why early Christian experiences led them to advocate a value system that differed from Judaism as well as becoming advocates of anti-Judaism.

Jews, regardless of whether they are secular Zionists or religious traditionalists are committed to and influenced by the events in Jewish history. The Torah, namely the Pentateuch describes God as a force that acts in history. Jewish holidays, with the exception of the High Holidays commemorate historical events such as the departure from Egypt, the giving of the Torah, life in the desert, and various victories and defeats. However, religious Jews and Zionists, treat history from a different perspective. To the religious Jews history continues to be the description of God in action and events in history are explained as consequences of God's will and judgment. Zionists contrarily see history as the consequence of power relationships, namely the consequences of human collectives in action. This is evident in how the Holocaust is viewed. For the ultra religious Jews, like present-day Chasidic Jews, the Holocaust is a punishment bestowed on Jews for disobeying God's commandments. For example Rabbi Ovadiah Yosef, the leader of the ultra-Orthodox Shass party in Israel declared that the Holocaust was indeed the punishment for disobedience to God's will. To Zionists and non-religious Jews, the Holocaust is the consequence of social forces influenced by a Christian anti-Jewish attitude derived from their faith and culture.

Of course I cannot discount the influence my Holocaust experiences had on my identity and world view. The Holocaust is but one incident, albeit a most devastating one, that Jews in the twentieth century experienced in the Christian world. There is a tendency among Jews to blame the rise of the Holocaust on the Nazi authoritarian mentality influenced by Hitler's psychosis. This tendency, however,

Faith and Conflict

obscures Christianity's direct contribution to the rise of European anti-Semitism.

Holocaust survivors, including me, carry in our consciousness the memories of the atrocities, the beatings and starvations that we experienced in the camps. These events have and continue to influence our world view of the Christian world. It was Pope Pius X who in a letter responding to Theodore Herzel's request that the Pope help to alleviate the suffering of the European Jews wrote: "Jews have not recognized our Lord therefore we cannot recognize the Jewish people."

In the last few years a number of books were published in which the authors propose that Christian theology has been instrumental in the development of European anti-Semitism. Constantine's anti-Jewish laws that were instituted in 350 C.E. have become a model for anti-Jewish laws and anti-Semitic perspectives. (See Carroll: Constantine's Sword). This was almost inevitable. In the process of developing its distinct identity as Christians and not another Jewish sect, Christian theology has become the anti-thesis to the Jewish thesis. In short, Christianity and Judaism have entered into a dialectical process. The sum of all dialectical stances is the encouragement of the separation of us from them and this dichotomization leads to a hostile stand between the two opponents. In the essays in this book I trace how this dialectical opposition is evident in the teachings of the Christian Bible.

The Holocaust is merely one, albeit the harshest treatment that Jews have experienced in the last two millennia. My participation in it reinforced my belief that the only place that Jews could be free from persecution be it Christian or Muslim is in their own land. My dream of Israel however was quite different from today's reality. Israel I have hoped would become the country of refuge, the place where Jews could find reprieve when any part of the world turns against them. Unlike Jews during the Holocaust atrocities who could not find refuge in other countries post World War II Jews who experienced hostilities in Islamic countries and Russia were able to leave those countries and find peace in Israel. Perhaps most of the representatives of the seventy odd nations that constituted the United Nations in 1947 who voted for the establishment of Israel must have held similar opinions. Such views may have arisen out of Western nations collective sense of guilt related to their countries contribution to the events that led to the destruction of European Jewry. Whatever the reason, the Holocaust was instrumental in the establishment of the Jewish homeland, Israel.

The Holocaust was my epiphany. It was my awakening to the continued existence of evil and inhumanity. This was also my realization that in spite of our advancement and evolution we are still governed by our inherent Id. But most importantly, it also showed me that religions that claim to be the guardians of universal morality have contrarily been the propagators of evil.

The question that I asked my father in the camp has continued to haunt me especially when I encounter the stories of continued atrocities that are referred to as "ethnic cleansing." The prevalence of ethnic cleansing and religious intolerance in Africa and Asia and my own experiences forces me to add another question to the one I asked my father. The question that I must ask is: What can be done to alleviate this prevailing inhumanity?

It stands to reason that after having experienced the pains and torture in the Holocaust I should be interested to find both the explanations and the solution for the historically recurring anti-Semitism. Most survivors, at least the many with whom I talked put the blame of the Holocaust on both the German character and their leadership especially Hitler. This is a narrow perspective. I seek to point out in my analysis that there are two separated issues. First, the need to understand how socio-economic conditions and the breakdown of expectations have led to fear which in turn incites aggression. And the second question is: why have Jews been chosen as the recipient of the negative sanctions especially in Europe? But the question of European hostilities toward Jews leads also to be critical of theology. Both Christian theologians

Faith and Conflict

and Jewish ones follow Job's friends view propose that the evil which besets people is due to God's will. I propose to debunk this view and propose that evil is a human creation. We create evil conditions and evil people and it is up to us and not God to fight evil.

Surely, it is time that we seek a cure for this human evil. While I taught courses in social problems I and many others have suggested that tolerance is the panacea for evil. But is it? I do not think so. So far, the teaching of tolerance had no impact on reducing intra-personal evil. Instead of tolerance, it is an adherence to justice that will impact on human inter-relationships. I propose that knowledge of the social forces that lead to anti-humanism and the teaching of justice rather than love and tolerance will have a far greater impact in eradicating the continually rising atrocities that we have and continue to experience in the post World War II world.

In my youth I planned to become a physician. To me it was the ideal profession. The knowledge and skills one has as a physician cannot be taken away and it provides the physician with the means to establish a comfortable life. This view was a response to my father's proposition that the single thing that no one can take away from us is knowledge. This, of course, is a philosophy that was derived from Jewish experiences of expulsions. After my liberation from the concentration camp I enrolled in the Charles University medical school in Prague. When it became evident that Czechoslovakia was turning into a communist country I escaped to Germany where I found employment as one of the social workers associated with the United Nation. Luckily, I also received a scholarship to come to study in the United States. I had hoped to continue my medical education. Instead of being admitted to medical school, I was told to enroll as an undergraduate student where I pursued a pre-med program. A year after my enrollment I was advised by the dean of foreign students who told me "Mr. Schoenfeld you are a foreign born Jew without any visible means of support. You do not have a chance to enter medical school." Again, even in this country, I faced injustice.

Sociology:

Early in my studies of sociology, I, like all graduate students, had to study Emile Durkheim, one of the founders of this discipline. Durkheim, who, like me, came from a long line of devout Jews, proposed views and theories that resonated with my views of the importance of justice In the Division of Labor, for instance, he declares that "[T]he task of the most advanced societies may therefore be said to be a mission for justice." (Division of Labor 321) He continues to tell us that "just as ancient peoples had above all a need for a common faith to live by, we have a need of justice. We can rest assured that this need will become ever more pressing if, as everything leads us to foresee, the conditions that dominate social evolution remain unchanged." (Division of Labor 322)

In this sense Durkheim sees, as did Feuerebach in The Essence of Christianity, his critical examination of religion, that faith in justice is more important in modern society than faith in a supernatural entity. Religious faith, especially when there is a great diversity of beliefs in a society, does not serve as an integrative force. To the contrary religious faith develops in the individual a sense of arrogance. The faithful person most often perceives himself to be a better person and more loved by God that those espousing other beliefs and in this manner faith continues to be a divisive and hostile force. If the modern world, like those in the past, seeks to find ways by which to establish a better and a more peaceful existence it must seek it not in religion or tolerance but in the principles of universal justice, namely, the principles of reciprocal rights and duties. This idea is the underlying common principle in my essays.

Perhaps my yearning for a just and humanitarian world was a response to a post Holocaust world in which anti-Jewish views continue to exist although they are sub rosa. For eighteen years (my whole existence before the Holocaust) I believed in the dictum: "Do not give

Faith and Conflict

Satan a cause to speak." I believed that if we Jews would hunker down, keep quiet and not cause trouble by demanding justice we will not give Christians cause to become hostile against us. By keeping quiet and not challenging the legitimacy of the Christian anti-Jewish teachings we have hoped not to anger Christians and thus avoid negative sanctions. In short, I was continually reminded: "Do not rock the boat, do not make weaves." We believed that by being invisible and by keeping quiet we will lessen the chances of hostile attacks against us. Even a cursory examination of European history shows the manifold Jewish tragedies such as expulsion from countries, killings and pogroms that began two millennia ago beginning with the anti-Jewish laws instituted by Constantine the Great that an emphasis on keeping quiet, to hold back one's tongue and temper, to disregard hurt and shame, and to withdraw as a puppy does in meekness did not have its desired effect. The Holocaust is evidence of the failure of being quiet. Still I continued to remain quiet. I did this even in the United States a country supposedly ruled by justice and freedom. I maintained the ingrained caution "not to give the Christians a reason to aggress against us." When occasionally I dared to differ from the established popular views I was frequently confronted with retorts such as: "If you do not like it here why don't you go back where you came from." It took me a long time to gain the courage to speak out, not to slink away, and not to turn the other cheek. I finally realized that I paid the price for my right to speak out even when my views would be contrary to popular beliefs and being critical of Christian religious teachings. The Holocaust was the price for my right to speak out.

From my Holocaust experiences I also learned that the philosophical perspective of keeping quiet and being invisible is not efficacious to the survival of Jews in a Christian world. Anti-Semitism exists independently of the behavior of Jews. For instance, German Jews who tried to assimilate into the Christian world and to become Christian- like in appearance and assume the mantle of middle class respectability

Sociology:

sadly learned that assimilation didn't work. Instead of being accepted German Jews instead found that they were accused of using it as a subterfuge to assume control over the country, at least over its economy. This, for instance is central in the Protocols of the Elders of Zion. Benjamin Disraeli, former British Prime Minister who converted from Judaism to Christianity, has often been referred to in derogatory terms as "the Jew." His conversion has been seen by many, especially by his English peers as being uppity. If on the other hand we kept ourselves apart from the other people and lived in self-imposed neighborhoods we were accused of being haughty and perceiving ourselves to be better than others and see ourselves as God's chosen people. Even conversion didn't work. Hitler and the Spanish Inquisition have shown that even those who converted could not shed their Jewish identity. The convert and his children, during the Nazi regime, were still considered and treated as Jews. Converts during the Inquisition were similarly perceived by the Catholic Church as untrue Catholics. They were called "conversos" or Marranos, pork eaters, a derogatory term. The converts' homes in many instances were marked with inverted crosses both as a sign of shame and as indication of being untrustworthy Catholics.

I have realized that there is a need to make people confront the evil that led to the Holocaust, an evil that continues to be a part of the human experience. In spite of the tragedies associated with World War II, people worldwide continue to create new "holocausts." In the last thirty years there were many forms of ethnic cleansing and tribal and religious wars which one could consider genocide. Whenever I lecture on the Holocaust I always tell the audience that I have not come to lecture because I seek sympathy either for myself or for the murdered six million Jews. Instead, I lecture in the hope that by sharing my experiences I can affect attitudes and views that may, even if in a minimal way, help alleviate inter ethnic, racial, and religious hostilities. In fact, I caution my audience that given the appropriate conditions, I believe, genocide could happen even in the United States. Now I lecture about

Faith and Conflict

my experiences because as a survivor and sociologist I wish to share my insights with others with the hope that my lectures may serve as a prophylaxis against the rise of "holocausts" in any form in the United States. I believe that people need to become aware of the conditions that can lead to the rejection of humanity and sanity in favor of intergroup hostility.

The essays in this volume are drawn from lectures that I delivered in the last ten years. Even when I do not write directly about a specific Holocaust experience, indirectly my views always reflect the influences of my Holocaust experiences. In some of my essays I seek to understand the forces that have contributed to two millennia of Christian hostility to Jews. In others I propose that in order to eliminate the chances of other "holocausts" there is a need to change our world views and especially our theology. After all, theological perspectives have had an impact not only on the justification of the Holocaust but on anti-Semitic acts beginning with the Constantine edicts of 350 C.E. to the present. To some, Jews and Christians alike, the content of my essays will appear controversial because I challenge both Jewish and Christian theological perspectives. I dare to express opinions that do not agree with either Christian or with traditional Jewish views. However, no progress can be achieved unless we begin with an open mind and are willing not to be blind to other points of views. Goodness is not reserved to one group of people nor is it a monopoly for any single theological perspective. We need to develop inter religious dialectics through which each religion can see and accept its own faults. We should not look at religion as the untouchable subject and hence not to be subject to honest criticism. In short, if we hope to eliminate inter-religious hostilities we must accept the legitimacy of honest criticism.

Old age has many undesirable traits. As much as I dislike my physical infirmities I must live with them. I am getting used to my physical limitations and accept them without bitterness although I still complain about them. Still there is one aspect to old age that is well expressed by a Talmudic saying: "Past eighty one acquires might." Of course, this statement does not refer to physical might but to personal courage to speak. Old age brings with it not only experience and insight but also the freedom to express them. Like I have told some people, at eighty five I am too old to be afraid.

Notes

1. The word Zionism is taken from the name of a hill in Israel (Zion) which in time became synonymous with Israel the country. References
2. Bialik Hayim N. and Ravnitzky Y.H. 1992 The Book of Legends (trans. W.G. Braude) N.Y. Schocken Books.
3. Carroll, James 2002 Constantine's Sword : The Church and the Jews New York, Houghton Mifflin
4. Durkheim, Emile 1984 The Division of Labor in Society (trans. W.D.Halls) The Free Press 4. Herzel, Theodore 1987 The Old New Land. Rbon House 24

Section II: The Causes of the Holocaust

Preface to Section Two: The Causes of the Holocaust

One of the oldest problems with which human beings were and continue to be concerned and for which they keep seeking an explanation is the existence of evil. Why is it that the wrong doers seem to flourish and prosper while the righteous people suffer? This is a central theme in the Bible. The redactors when editing The Bible devoted a whole book, the book of Job, in which the author seeks to find an explanation for it.

The magnitude of evil was so great in the Holocaust that the world and especially the survivors cry out in frustration "why?" Was the Holocaust the will of this inscrutable God who supposed to control everything that occurs in this universe? Or, is evil a human creation and not wishing to take responsibility for it we merely transfer all causes to God and washing our hands from the evil we proclaim: Who among us can understand the mysteries of God? In the first essay I examine the three theodecies, namely the religious explanations we created by which we attempt to give reason for the existence of evil and the seeming injustices in the allocation of rewards and punishments. Of course

Faith and Conflict

the Holocaust is a classic example in which the righteous and the sinners, the just and the unjust have suffered almost equally. In fact, in the concentration camps justice failed for the most brutal inmates were selected for supervisory positions and as a reward for their brutality they received more food and power and thereby assuring their survival. And yet many still propose as an answer: God must have had a reason.

The problem of religious explanation of evil is that it is based on faith. One accepts God's will simply because God is, even when it seems contrary, always just. People accept on faith God's righteousness and we proclaim now as the author of book of Job did: God must have His reasons but we may not understand them. Perhaps neither prayer nor faith; neither magic nor amulets will avert the existence of evil.

If we wish to understand the causes of evil and be able to control that scourge of evil we must look at the problem from a scientific perspective which places its existence on life choices we make.

In the second essay I propose that the social conditions under which evil which I see as the absence of justice, is the result of our actions and not that of God. We are responsible both for goodness and harmony as well as evil and pain. We cannot alter and improve this world unless we accept our responsibility for our actions. In this instance the only way that leads us to understand why the Holocaust existed is to examine the social conditions that leads people in a society give up their freedom of thought, to reject the essentiality of justice, and to select groups of people for unjust treatment. It is only when we accept that evil is a human construct rather than God's will can we affect and alter the social forces that have always been the underpinnings for the rise of evil.

Causes of the Holocaust
A Religious Perspective

A young woman attending my course on the sociology of religion asked me: "Professor! Why does God permit evil to exist?" She asked me not only because I was a professor of sociology of religion but, also because she knew that I was a survivor of the Holocaust.

Those who asked me such a question, and there were others among those who attend my talks on my Holocaust experiences, seek to ascertain how, I as a survivor, who lost his family, whose life was destroyed, still could believe in God's existence. Most who ask me this or similar questions about God and the existence of evil do so because life confronts them with this seeming paradox: How can God, who is supposed to be all merciful, all loving, and forgiving entity permit, if not directly ordain the existence of evil?

The existence of evil is of course frightening. But, what is even more frightening is the idea that God, who in our view is our protector from evil and whom we trust as our champion to defeat the masters of evil, be they human or transcendental entities like Satan, is Himself a possible cause for the existence of Evil.

For us Jews of the twentieth century the ultimate of all evils was the Holocaust. Therefore, how is it possible that God permitted the existence of the Holocaust in which millions of Jews were killed with whom, according to traditional Jewish belief, God has had a special

Faith and Conflict

relationship and to whom God has referred as his people? I was told of a rabbi who, when liberated by the Russian army from a concentration camp borrowed a soldier's gun and began shooting it heavenward. When asked what he was doing he replied: "I want to kill God." I suppose that this rabbi felt, like many Jews did, that God violated his holy covenant with his people and thereby God has violated the fundamental principle advocated in the Torah – the principle of justice.

The existence of evil has always been problematic to those who believe in God's goodness and in his total commitment to moral principle of justice. Jewish and Christian theologies alike proclaim in diverse ways that God as the king of the universe is the cause of all causes. Therefore evil cannot exist unless God himself permits its existence and thereby violate his own moral law.

The first of Maimonides' thirteen principles of faith declares: I firmly believe that the Creator, blessed be his name, is the Creator and Ruler of all created beings, and that He alone has made, does make, and ever will make all things. Similarly St. Augustine and Thomas de Aquinas declared that God is the first cause and that He is the cause of all causes. Nothing, we are taught, occurs outside of his will. This view is, for example, central in the Jewish Holy Day prayers. In the orthodox and conservative synagogues during the Mussaf services (added services) the congregation recites a prayer U'Nessane Tokef composed by Rabbi Amnon in which the author proclaims that on this day (i.e. Rosh Hashanah and Yom Kippur) God decides who shall live and who shall die and the manner in which the person will die. Similarly, on these Holy Days with Torah ark opened symbolically representing the extreme significance of the prayer to be recited, the congregation beseeches God with the following prayer: "Our Father our King inscribe us in the book of good life." All the prayers on the Holy Days of New Year and the Day of Atonement have one central theme – a belief that on these days God, the supreme judge and king, determines the fate of all people, Jews and non-Jews alike. If we accept this perspective of

Causes of the Holocaust A Religious Perspective

God then we must also accept the view that the Holocaust could not have happened outside of His will. Hence, the faithful can rightfully ask: What kind of God do we worship? Isn't there an inconsistency in our religious belief system that on the one hand it advocates that God is just and merciful and on the other hand that He also decrees such evil as the Holocaust? Throughout the Torah, the Prophets and the poets in the Book of Psalms and perhaps in all the writings that cumulatively we call the Bible (T'nach) we are repeatedly reminded that God is both just and merciful. We Jews are also taught to accept as a matter of faith that God is a just and moral God who rewards the righteous and punishes the wicked. In Psalm 145 (known as Ashrei) we recite that God is just and righteous in all his acts, that God guards all those who love him and destroys all the evildoers.

But, if God's character reflects His commitment to justice, mercy, and compassion how could He have permitted, or perhaps even ordained, the destruction of millions of people? Is this view not contrary to Biblical insistence that God does not permit for evil to flourish nor does He let the just to suffer? If so, then the belief that God is the destroyer of evil seems to be false. How can we accept the truth of the belief of God as the all just entity when on the one hand, He demands that humans be committed to justice and morality but on the other hand He seems to exclude himself from selfsame moral requirements? Indeed the Romans may have been right when they coined the statement: Quod licet Jovi non licet Bovi. (What Jupiter is allowed to do the ox may not.) If the Roman saying is true then the rabbinical teaching that God and people are equally bound to the moral teaching of the Torah is fallacious. Why has God departed from the moral requirements that He seeks in us? If indeed He is a just God how could He have permitted, if not directly decreed, the existence of the Holocaust?

To examine this issue I need to define first evil. Evil, in my view, are those collective and individual human acts that deprive others of their inalienable right not only to life but also to a quality of life. Most

Faith and Conflict

human beings perceive that they have a right to life and to a degree comfort in life. In his study of the social causes of suicide Durkheim declares that "at every moment of history there is a dim perception in the moral consciousness of societies, of the respective value of different social services, the relative reward due to each, and the consequent degree of comfort appropriate on the average to workers in each occupation."(Durkheim, 1966 p.249) If, a society deprives people of their right to life, to work, and to their legitimate comfort then such a society performs acts of evil. From this perspective evil exists when injustice flourishes. Sodom and Gomorrah and Nineveh were evil cities because they abhorred justice. Of course deprivation of life and comfort can be caused by either human acts or by nature that is what people consider to be an act of God. But can an act of God, that is a natural calamity, also be considered to be evil? In some sense people do feel justified to define even such acts as evil: that is, as acts of injustice. To alleviate this bothersome discrepancy between our views of God's benevolence and the existence of evil religions have constructed a set of theodecies, that is, theologically accepted explanations why evil exists. Theodecies propose that what we consider evil may not be so, but are legitimate and justified actions by God. But this view has a major flaw: when theodecies justify God for the existence of evil they at the same time also absolve human beings who perpetrate evil from the sin of the evil that they commit. For instance, the statement that is recited when a person dies "God gives and God takes away blessed be the name of God" serves to justify and legitimate death not as a natural phenomenon but as an act of God's judgment

In Judaism the theodecies, namely the theological explanations for the existence of evil incorporate the following three themes. First it proposes that what we perceive as evil is merely the way God tests us, second, that evil exists as a punishment for wrong doing, and third, that because of our ignorance of God's ways we are unable to understand God's purpose and intent that sometimes seem to appear as evil acts. All these explanations, especially the last one, require that we accept with utmost faith the dictum that what God does is always for the best.

Let me begin by examining the first theodecy that proposes: What we may consider evil is often a test through which God seeks to ascertain a person's degree of faith – they are Nissayonos (tests). In Genesis we are told that God wished to test Abraham's faith and thus He asked Abraham to sacrifice his son Isaac. In fact, it is said (Bialik and Ravintzky, 1992) that Abraham was tested in ten different ways. But so great was his love of God that he passed all ten tests. Similarly, in a response to a dare proposed by Satan God permitted the latter to test Job's steadfastness of faith by permitting Satan to subject Job to all sorts of evil. Hence, those whose faith is strong and unwavering will pass the imposed test and will merit future reward. How often do we hear that a possible reason why a person becomes ill is that it is God's way to test the extent to which the tested person has a steadfast faith in God.

The difficulty I have with this theodicy, and I am sure there are many who share my question: Why does God need to tests us at all? As a teacher I tested most of my students because I had to give them a grade that is based on proving that they studied and have acquired a certain degree of knowledge of the subject I taught. Not being clairvoyant I had to test them. But isn't God unlike us humans? Unlike God I as a teacher am not endowed with insight and unlimited information of my students. But unlike human beings God, as some of the Jewish prayers inform us, can penetrate our mind and soul and hence know the innermost recesses of our hearts (chadrey k'layoth)? Maimonides included this idea as one of the thirteen principles of the Jewish faith. Each Jew he proposes "should believe with a perfect faith that the Creator, blessed be His name, knows every deed the children of men, and all their thoughts." After all doesn't God fashion the hearts of humans? Being an all knowing entity He must be aware even without

Faith and Conflict

testing the degree of each person's sincerity of faith. If we accept the belief in the existence of an all knowing God, we must also accept that God is aware without having to test whether one's faith is genuine and intrinsic or false and extrinsic. Is He so uncertain of our state of faith that He needs to test us and make us prove to Him or even to ourselves our unwavering faith by overcoming obstacles that He deliberately places in front of us as temptations and stumbling blocks? In our legal system when the prosecution deliberately tempts us to violate the law, we consider such acts as entrapment which is both illegal and immoral. Is God so unsure of His knowledge of us that He needs to resort to the type of action that we humans, even with our frail understanding of justice, consider it not only illegal but also immoral? Does He not uphold His own moral injunction that states: "Thou shall not curse the deaf, nor put a stumbling block before the blind...?" Isn't, God's act of placing people in jeopardy inconsistent with the Jewish idea that God accepted the rule of justice and that He must be abeyant to the selfsame laws that He demands of people? To most educated person's mind it is inconceivable that God can be such a petty tyrant who for his own elucidation puts not only stumbling blocks in front of his creations but permits or ordains their death just so that He can test the faithfulness of his presumed followers. The idea that God needs to test his adherents is to me preposterous. But it is even more ludicrous to assume that God wishes to test children who have not yet developed a moral consciousness and do not know right from wrong. I for one cannot accept such an explanation and would propose that it should be omitted from modern theology as an explanation of evil. Indeed, I cannot accept that the Holocaust in which millions of innocent people died was a test ordained by God.

Let me now turn to the next theodecy namely, that evil exists as punishment for wrong doing. I have heard quite often this threat: "God will get you for this." In my early teens I disobeyed my mother's wishes. I wanted to play soccer in an organized school league. My mother, a typical orthodox Jewish woman from a small village, was fearful of sports. Somewhere she heard that soccer players end up with enlarged hearts and of course early death. Regardless of my arguments against her fallacious view of sports she remained adamant against my participation in soccer. I disobeyed her and shortly after my first game my foot became infected. I went to my uncle "the doctor" he squeezed the infected area and with it he drained the puss. His comments were classical: "God punished you for disobeying your mother."

Fear of God is one of the central themes in religion. One of the first ideas that I was taught in religious school that "the beginning of wisdom is the fear of God."(Proverbs 1:7) Even though Christianity proclaims that God is love it also stresses the centrality of punishment for sins that people commit. One of the founding elements in Christian faith is that people still suffer because of the original sin. Both Judaism and Christianity propose that people can be punished in this life as well as in the next one. A person can be punished by torments of body or of soul both in this world and by losing salvation in the next world. (In the Jewish theology loss of salvation is expressed as a person's loss of his portion in the world to come.) In Leviticus 26.14 we encounter the passage that in Hebrew is named the "Tocheycha" the warning. In it God warns the people of Israel that if they act contrarily to His commandments and if they will not heed His words then His wrath will be poured out against them. The passage outlines the evil things that will befall the people from agricultural disasters to being subjugated by the enemies. The list of disasters sounds almost like the ten plagues that God brought on Egypt. The text describes it as follows: "I will bring seven times more plagues upon you according to your sins. And I will send the beast of the field among you, which shall rob you of your children, and destroy your cattle, and make you few in number; and your ways shall become desolate." The text continues with the description of calamities and informs us that God "will bring a sword upon you, that shall execute the vengeance of the covenant ... and ye shall be delivered

Faith and Conflict

into the hands of the enemy." Finally Jews will suffer from hunger there will be an absence of food so that" ten women shall bake bread in one oven ... and ye shall eat, and not be satisfied." The eleventh principle of faith enunciated by Moses Maimonides states "I believe with perfect faith that the Creator, blessed be his Name, rewards those that keep his commandments, and punishes those that transgress them."

Indeed the threat of being punished for violating the Mitzvoth (the commandments) has been an all pervasive belief in Judaism. The idea that God punishes those who violate his commandments was and continues to be an accepted dictum. Hasn't God punished the people of Sodom and Gomorrah? When Job, for instance, lost his family, wealth and health his friends advised him to confess his sins and God will perhaps forgive him and will spare him from any additional punishments. In fact Eliphaz the Temanite puts a positive spin on punishment. First he assures Job that no one perishes by the hand of God unless he is guilty. So, if Job is innocent, as he claims to be, he will escape from any further punishment although being punished is in fact a sign that God cares about the punished person. "Behold" he states "happy is the man whom God corrects" because after having been punished God binds up the wounds and His hands make will redeem you from death. The Prophets have often declared that the destruction of Israel, Judea and the Temple were punishments for the sins committed by the Jews. We are also told, however, that God doesn't punish the righteous with the transgressors. When God revealed to Abraham his plan to destroy Sodom and Gomorrah Abraham inquired: Wilt Thou indeed sweep away the righteous with the wicked?" In the ensuing bargaining between Abraham and God he promised Abraham that He will not destroy the city if there would be at least ten righteous individuals. Yet, the Holocaust was an event where the righteous and the sinful, the young and the innocent together with the elderly and the guilty died in the same gas chamber. There are still Jews, like Rabbi Ovadiah Yosef, the leader of the ultra-orthodox Shass party in Israel who continues to claim that the Holocaust was a punishment ordained by God the sins of the Jews. This Rabbi reminds me of the rabbi in my synagogue in my home town who on Yom Kippur (Day of Atonement) afternoon in a wailing voice was predicting an onslaught of punishments because the more modern women were violating the laws of ritual purity when they went to the Mikvah (ritual bath) with their hair unshorn. Such or very similar view is also central in orthodox Christianity. How did Jerry Falwell and Pat Robertson explained the 9/11 tragedy? They proclaimed "that God was mad at Americans because it harbored feminists, gays, and civil libertarians." (Newsweek vol.148:47) Hasn't Pat Robertson predicted that the Illinois town that voted against the teaching of creationism will be severely punished by God? Christians and Jews alike are more concerned with God's anger rather than God's love. In fact Newsweek polls show that in 1999 49 per cent of Americans would have voted for an atheist for president but after 9/11 it dropped to 37 per cent.

Were I to accept the idea of that God punishes those who sin, I would limit my definition of sin as the violation of the moral laws of justice. I would not define sin as Orthodox Jews do as the violation of ritual laws, nor would I equate it with the absence of faith as Christians do. Sodom and Gomorrah were destroyed because they were immoral cities, namely, the Sodomites rejected the fundamental moral laws of justice and mercy. The great city Ninevah (whom the Prophets called the Bloody City) was also threatened with destruction because of their immorality and not because of their lack of belief in the one and true God. None of these cities were either threatened to be punished or were punished for their lack of performance of prescribed ritual laws. The calamities that the most Biblical prophets were predicting were not for lack of ritual observance. Punishment was in their view the consequence of immorality which in their view was associated with lacking concern for their fellow men. I propose that from a theological perspective one could argue that the destruction of Nazi Germany was the

Faith and Conflict

result of their immorality. Jews suffered the outrageous calamities not because lack of ritual observances, nor, because of their refusal to accept Christ, as some orthodox Christians would like us to believe.

The idea that God punishes the collective for the sins of individuals, even though they are many individuals, is not the view that is given us in the Bible. Consider the following episode described in the book of Genesis (18:25) Abraham, the father of monotheism argues with God on account of His desire to destroy Sodom and Gomorrah. Abraham reminds God of His essence as he states "That be it far for Thee to do after this manner, to slay the righteous with the wicked, so that the righteous be as the wicked; that be far from Thee; shall not the judge of all the earth do justly?" The Jewish point of view is that God is subject to the same laws of justice that He expects from humans. I cannot believe that the Holocaust and 9/11 where the just and the unjust have died together is an act of God. For instance, what sins could have been committed by my brother at age thirteen and my sister at ten who were killed in the Holocaust?

Jews were killed in the Holocaust, just as the three thousand persons who were killed in 9/11 simply because evil exists independently of God. It is not logical to accept a belief that God who is the source of all morality will deliberately perform immoral acts and the Holocaust was the epitome of immoral acts. I cannot accept the idea that the Holocaust was God's punishment for Jews' assumed violation of ritual laws as Rabbi Ovadiah Yosef has stated or the perspectives advocated by Reverends Falwell and Robertson. To accept the idea that the Holocaust and 9/11 were God's punishment for the wickedness of both those who died and those suffered because of their death must ipso facto casts doubt on God's fairness, his mercifulness, and above all his sense of justice.

Finally the third theodecy proposes that we cannot explain the existence of evil because we cannot understand God's ways and His reasons for allowing seemingly evil conditions to exist. In the past,

Jews, like most Christians and Muslims, have had an abiding faith that God is always perfect and His perfection is also evident in His unquestioned justice. Jews, for instance, have responded to personal tragedies with the saying "this too is for the best." This reflects the commonly accepted view that we mortals cannot understand God's intent and purpose. Hence we must accept the idea that a person's suffering is in an unknown way essentially good, even though, at the moment we the sufferers cannot ascertain its goodness. This view is founded in God's response to Job when he sought to make sense of and seek understanding why he is suffering. In the story God answers Job when he seeks to understand all that is happening to him by declaring that His reasons are not known to humans and that people, because of their lack of knowledge and understanding, must accept that whatever happens in their life on faith alone. Speaking out of a whirlwind God thunders: Where were you when I laid the foundations of the earth? Declare, if you have the understanding. Who determined the measures thereof fastened? In short God tells us that we as mere humans lack the understanding the reason for his deeds. (Job 38:4-6)

Religion demands that we accept God on faith alone and that we do not have the right to judge His actions nor inquire into the unknown and unknowable and therefore God's actions must be taken to be just on faith alone. Even in the face of death Jews are required to declare: **Blessed is the true judge.** (Emphasis added by author.) When something undesirable happens I was taught to say submissively "this too is for the best."

In my youth I was indoctrinated in the belief that even when we cannot always comprehend the reasons of God's actions. This view was reinforced in me with the following legend. In his frequent conversation with God, David complained to Him about the pesky mosquitoes that pestered him. God wished to show David that although human beings may not understand His purpose there is a good and valid reason for what He has done and created. David was brought to realize this

Faith and Conflict

with the following incident. When David was hiding from King Saul who wanted to kill him, he devised a plan of action through which he hoped to show Saul that in spite of the persecutions he endured from him he is, none the less is a loyal subject. One night when Saul and his army slept David stealthily entered the camp. His plan was to cut off a corner of the king's garment and show it to him the next morning. In this manner David hoped to prove to Saul that were he truly his enemy he could have easily killed him – but he did not. As David started to execute his plan lying next to Saul and preparing to cut of the corner of Saul's garment Saul turned in his sleep and put his massive leg on top of David and thereby made his escape from the camp impossible. David, the legend tells us, prayed to God and in response God ordained a mosquito to bite Saul's leg who reacted instinctively by moving his leg thus facilitating David's escape. The grateful David, who was also known as the "sweet singer" wrote the poem that is now included in the Psalms in which he declares: How great are your deeds Oh Lord you created them all in your wisdom.

The central problem in all three theodecies is that they relieve the evil doer from the responsibility of his deeds. After all, the common denominator in the three theodecies is that whatever happens to us or to the world is ordained by God. Therefore when a person commits an evil act he is not responsible for it, his actions are pre-ordained.

The actor has no responsibility for his action; his actions are compelled by God and therefore he cannot be blamed for his deed. After all, people are pawns in God's hands they are slaves to His will. The evil doer is merely fulfilling his ordained destiny. As my grandmother would have said "vuss ist beshert is beshert," namely what has been foreordained is foreordained. If we accept any of the above explanations for the existence of evil, then we must also accept the preposterous idea that Hitler was merely God's instrument. Just as Pharaoh's heart was hardened by God in order to serve His own purposes, so one could argue, Hitler's heart too, was hardened by God and therefore he had no other recourse but to fulfill his preordained destiny.

I cannot accept any of these theodecies as valid explanation for the existence of evil in general and for the Holocaust in particular. There is a difference between accepting God as a universal force and as a source of wisdom that helps us to distinguish between good and evil from an anthropomorphic God who not only micro manages the human world but who gets angry and jealous and often people must bear the brunt of his anger.

I can understand our desire for wanting a human like God. After all if we accept the view that God can be described by human attributes then it follows that we can use the same means to influence God as we do to influence human beings who are in super-ordinate positions. We can beg, cajole, promise gifts and thusly influence God to change the evil and undesirable conditions that He may have ordained against us. Didn't Moses try to influence God by attempting to shame Him? Didn't he declare to God "What will the Egyptians say if you destroy the Jews? This is almost like we say "what will the neighbors say?" However, when we humanize God we also rob God of his transcendental spiritual essence. Rabbi Kushner in his now famous book When Bad Things Happen to Good People has eloquently argued against the prevailing anthropomorphic view of God. To him the existence of what we call natural evil is independent of God. They are random events and are not preordained by God. This of course proposes that natural disasters, including illness, although undesirable occur due to natural laws that are independent of God.

The perception of evil as God's punishment was always softened by our belief and hope that there are ways to gain redemption and avert any evil decree. From the Jewish point of view evil can always be eradicated by "tfilah, tshuvah, and tzedakah" by prayer, by returning to correct way of live and by charitable acts. The threat of punishment was efficacious in making people adhere to laws. Such a view held sway with

Faith and Conflict

my parents and grandparents however today it merely serves as another reason for the educated and secularized people to reject religion as an explanation of tragedies. We need a new theology one that eliminates God as the cause of all occurrences and instead accepts the notion that this world in which we live is a human world and much of the evil we experience are a function of human action alone.

To look at evil from a modern perspective we must begin by separating the natural world from the human world. Of course there are undesirable events in both worlds but evil exists only in the human world. We must also distinguish between tragedies and evil. Tragedies are undesirable and catastrophic events that are part of the natural world. They are undesirable because they produce illness, pain, and death, namely conditions that are detrimental to human existence and comfort. They are not evil in themselves, because the events were not deliberately directed against a targeted population. (Of course when human beings change the natural conditions, that is, they disregard nature's laws then we may declare that such conditions were produced by evil.) Earthquakes, hurricanes, and tornadoes often destroy property, human comfort and human life but because they are natural and predictable events they are not acts evil in themselves. The deaths and havoc they create are not deliberate. We can, to a large extent, protect ourselves from these tragedies simply by moving away from areas that are most likely to have such occurrences. If, however, I chose to live on a fault line I do so with my understanding that I will be subject to earthquakes. The great tragedies, the pandemics that human beings were subjected to during the Middle Ages such as the Black Death, small pox, cholera, typhus, and others are tragedies but they are not evil because they are not the deliberate consequences of acts of evil people. The cyclical occurrences of draught and hunger are neither evil nor are they forms of God's punishment for our evil ways. They are responses to natural conditions. Evil is neither the handiwork of transcendental figures such as Satan, the Devil, or Beelzebub. Evil is purely a human construct. It is a concept that that defines all human actions that are deliberately directed to hurt other human beings. Tragedies, unlike evil deeds, are not immoral they are not the consequences of violation of morals.

I would like to propose that the reason for evil can be ascertained only if we accept the proposition that both evil and goodness are part of our social world which in itself is a human construct. The human world and all that is contained in it is a world that has neither been established by nor foreordained by God. The human world is not a "natural" world – it is a human creation. This view is not contrary to traditional Jewish teachings. To the contrary it is rooted in it. We are told in Genesis that after God created mankind He proclaimed: be fruitful, multiply and have dominion over the earth. This passage fits very well with the rabbinical concept "tzimtzum" i.e., God's shrinkage.

Cabalistic legend teaches us that when God decided to create the universe, it was filled with His presence and there was no room into which a world could be created. God, therefore, shrunk and withdrew Him/ Herself and in this void He created the world (or universe). Having removed Him/Herself from the space in which a human world was created He/She then turned it over to mankind to have dominion over it. One of the psalmists has expressed this idea thusly: "The heaven is the Lord's heaven, but the earth was given to mankind." (Psalm 115:16) Once we acquired dominion over the world, it becomes our task to rule and make the world a human world. It is in such a world — a world ruled by humans — that the concept "tikun olam" (the Jewish conception that it is mankind's duty to improve the world) makes sense. The idea of Tikun Olam reflects the Jewish conception of man's purpose in this world. Contrary to Christian view the Jewish view of creation proposes that God deliberately left the world unfinished so that humans are given an opportunity to become God's partner in the continual process of creating and re-creating the world. It is the duty of every human being to continually improve (tikun) the world by

Faith and Conflict

making it a just world. This is how I interpret the passage that states that God turned over the dominion of the world to Adam, who is but the symbol of humankind.

The idea that this world is a human world is also evidenced in the following Talmudic tale. (Talmud "Baba Mezia" p.59b) This tale tells us that Rabbi Eliezer and the sages (most likely members of the Sanhedrin) had a heated discourse regarding the cleanliness of a particular oven (i.e. its acceptability as being Kosher.) Rabbi Eliezer sought to prove that his perspective is right through heavenly power. "If the Halachah (traditional law that is considered to be also given by God) agrees with me said Rabbi Eliezer let this carob-tree prove it. Thereupon the carob-tree was torn a hundred cubits out of its place. The sages refused to accept this as proof that Rabbi Eliezer is correct. Then Rabbi Eliezer sought to prove the correctness of his point of view by making the stream nearby flow backward and still further he made the walls of the house of study bend inwards threatening to burry its occupants. Still the sages refused to acquiesce to his view. Finally, the Rabbi asked that God Himself declare his rightness. Then a heavenly voice declared that Rabbi Eliezer is correct. Whereupon Rabbi Joshua, a member of the sages, declared: "Lo bashamayim hee" the law is not in heaven. It was his view, one that is accepted in Judaism, that is spite of the heavenly voice declaring Rabbi Eliezer correct the law is no longer in heaven. By this Rabbi Joshua meant, said Rabbi Jeremiah that while the law was given by God at Mount Sinai, once given any further interpretation of it belongs to those given by the rabbinical majority. In short the law like our world is a human product. (Talmud Baba Metziah p.38)

This is our world. It is we, and not God, who are morally bound to improve it by adhering to the principles of justice given by God but interpreted by society. Since this is our world, a human world, we and not God who are responsible for all that occurs in it – whether good or bad. It is our choice and therefore as God instructs us: let us chose life and not death; let us chose goodness instead of evil; let us create a moral world instead an immoral one. Evil is not the absence of good. Evil is the deliberate choice of action by some persons or a whole society that subjects others to pain and death and the denial of one's right to a happy life.

Of course we were not left without some guidance how to live and rule our world. We were given the two principles that are the foundation of a moral world. They are justice and mercy. When we violate these two principles we create evil. Adherence to or the rejection of these principles is not predetermined or preordained by God. They are choices that we make based on our free will. God has nothing to do whether a person or a nation is righteous or evil. The righteous person is one who accepts and observes the rights of others, thereby adheres to the principle of justice. By and large the principle of justice requires that all people be given equal access to life. When we deprive others from having an access to their life chances, when we practice injustice, we create evil. Mercy that accompanies justices is also one of God's main attribute. Mercy is love in action. Mercy arises out of our ability to love another as ourselves to emphasize with others, to be able to place oneself in the other's place and understand his action from his point of view. It is this that the Torah really means when it declares God's word: Behold I give you today good and evil, life and death, therefore chose life.

From this point of view the actions that created the Holocaust were the consequence of free choices of one man (Hitler) and his nation. Both he and his actions are evil because they rejected the foundation of morality of the principles of justice and mercy. We cannot blame God for its occurrence. It was purely the result of decisions and choices by some evil people.

Faith and Conflict

References:

1. Babylonian Talmud Baba Mezia The Schottenstein Hebrew Edition
2. Berenbaum, Michael The World Must Know N.Y. Shapolosky
3. Bialik Hayim N. and Ravintzki Y.H. 1992 The Book of Legends N.Y Shoken Books
4. Durkheim, Emile, 1966 Suicide New York, The Free Press
5. Lessing, Gotthold E. 2004 Nathan the Wise Boston St,. Martin Press
6. Luther, Martin 2008 The Jews and their Lies Kindle edition
7. Sartre, Jean Paul 1976 "The Flies" in No Exist and three other plays Vinge Internation
8. The Holy Bible : Job 38:4-6 43

The Holocaust:
A Sociological Perspective

The question that I seek to answer in this essay is the same question that I asked my father after I have been the recipient of an unjustified beating by the hands of a Kapo is: "How is it possible that today in the middle of twentieth century with all the moral advancements in understanding history, morals, ethics, and philosophy supposedly attesting to the advancement of mankind we are still so inhumane to each other?"

Of course religion has attempted to explain the reason for the existence of evil. However, theological explanations, as I proposed in the earlier chapter, do not provide testable hypotheses they are merely ways by which theologians seek to justify God's actions.

It seems that in spite of the religious teaching and its moral ideals, we still cannot, or perhaps will not conquer the evil inside of us. Far too often we revert to our original nature and we let the naked ape the "Id" dominate us and control our attitudes and behavior.

Is it possible that our civility is merely a thin and a transparent veneer that we use to cover, albeit inadequately, our aggressive nature? Is the Christian perspective valid that man's true nature is fundamentally evil? Is it true, as Christianity seeks to teach us, that when left to our own devices we cannot perfect ourselves? Must we accept the idea that we have not and cannot achieve social progress because our inherent aggressiveness? Is our nature really reflected by Cain when he slew Abel?

Faith and Conflict

In spite of all the evil that the Jewish people as well as many other nations who had experienced during the last two millennia I refuse to reject my belief in human perfectibility. Instead of the negative view expounded in Christian theology I choose to hold on to the Jewish perspective resplendent in the rabbinic philosophy that advocates the belief in human perfectibility. I choose to believe that we can achieve a Messianic period in which mankind will eliminate war and every one will live in safety and none shall be afraid. Of course I do not accept the veracity of my mother's dream that one day God in his wisdom will send us David or one of his descendants who will appear on a white horse bedecked in great splendor who will create a new world of plenty. These are unachievable dreams or as Sigmund Freud Called them "Shnorer Treume" (Beggars dreams). I do believe, however, that if we wish it, a peaceful world can be achieved by us. To paraphrase Theodor Herzl's dictum when he dreamt of a Jewish State, if we but will it our wishes and dreams can become a reality.

As one would expect, the memory of the beatings I received in Auschwitz and in the other concentration camps have never left me. Even when I have forgotten many other unhappy events, some of the tortures will never be erased from my consciousness. I guess my encounter with evil was personified by the Nazi's inhumanity and that left an indelible mark on my psyche. These memories became a significant part of my existential consciousness. None the less, I still refuse to become cynical and give up my belief in human perfectibility – either as individuals or as collectives. I will continue to hold on to my hope of the advent of a better world, one enunciated in the visions of both Micah and Isaiah. It is this hope that I believe was an instrumental force of Jews survival in spite of two millennia of atrocities. It was this hope that kept Jews, even in times of great desperation, to maintain a yearning for and a firm belief in our eventual return to the Jewish ancestral land. No wonder that the Jewish national anthem is an ode to hope. It is hope that even today leads me to seek the means by which we can alleviate, if not necessarily eradicate, the dominance of that part of human nature which Jewish theology refers to as "Yetzer Harah" the evil inclination and which was designated by Freud as the "Id" the source of human tragedies.

In the last two decades I have become involved with Holocaust education. I have spoken on many occasions to various high school and college classes as well as to civic groups. I tell the audiences, that my intent is neither to elicit sympathy for the Jews who were killed in the Holocaust nor am I seeking sympathy for those who survived it. Rather, I have taken on the obligation to teach by relating my experiences, even though it is both physically and emotionally difficult for me. I do this because I hope that through education I can allay my fear of the possible repetition of the Holocaust. My concern about the maintenance of our freedoms in the United States especially those of free expression, and of religion. This wish was intensified in me by the McCarthy period that sometime came very close to a Nazi philosophy. Even after my liberation from the concentration camp and now residing in the United States I still feel threatened. I am fearful that my new adopted home will in the face of economic difficulties loose the ideals on which it was built. I feel threatened by the demand on ideological conformity and the expression of politically correct ideologies. I remember well this stress when as a substitute teacher in a high school I dared to propose that while I strongly oppose communism I cannot discard all of Marx's ideas because some of his views of the affects of the economic infrastructure have on ideology is valid. If we in the United States wish to be immune to the forces that led the Germans to create the Holocaust and the many atrocities committed by other nations in the last two millennia we must understand not only our human weaknesses but, and even more important, to be aware of the social conditions that can be exploited by evil leaders in their desire to acquire power. However, in order to immunize ourselves from charismatic leaders who propagate immoral ideals we must also face our own weaknesses, namely, that like other nations we too when given certain economic conditions, may wish to escape from freedom and become subservient to moral charlatans.

Faith and Conflict

The only way that we can hope to eliminate holocaust like conditions from happening in the United States is to become aware of the conditions that are associated with the rise of evil totalitarian governments. Only then can we be on guard and avoid being subject to a totalitarian regime. I propose therefore to examine the nature of society and its culture and seek within it both the causes and the solution to inter-group hostilities. We must become aware of those conditions that generate the fears which, I believe, lead to the rejection of personal freedom, and accept conditions that subvert rational thinking and subjugate the human instincts for justice and for those ideals that are necessary to make us not only human but more importantly thy make us into humane beings. We must examine and understand the content of our culture especially our beliefs that often legitimate and perhaps even advocate genocide as a solution to social problem. Because of my personal experiences in the Holocaust and historical Christian hostilities of Jews in Europe I will limit my explanation to what I consider to have led to the genesis of the Holocaust. The theories that I present in this essay are rooted both in my Holocaust experiences and in sociological theory. In spite of the absence of a disciplined scholarship this essay might none the less be helpful in understanding not only the rise of the Holocaust but also acts of genocide in general.

Chaos and Fear:

Let me begin by proposing that the Holocaust like all inter-group aggression such as ethnic cleansing have arisen out fear usually brought on by the breakdown of the established moral order and normative expectations. This proposition is rooted in Durkheim's theory of anomie presented in his classical study Suicide (Durkheim, 1951). One of the factors that affect rates of suicide in a society, Durkheim proposes, is associated with the rise and fall of a country's economy.

These are the times, Durkheim proposes, when morals that control human appetites and greed break down. He called this condition "anomie." No living being" Durkheim proposes can be happy or even exist unless his needs are sufficiently proportioned to his means. In other words, if one's needs or desires which a person considers necessary for his legitimate life style are less than those he can legitimately obtain, he will experience a continual psychological friction and can only function painfully. (Durkheim, 1951 p.246) Therefore, Durkheim proposes "to achieve any other result, the passions first must be limited. Only then can they be harmonized with the faculties and satisfied." There is nothing in the human psyche or in the human physiology that provides a built in control for desires. Such forces exist only exterior to the human being. (Durkheim 1951 p.248) To Durkheim this exterior force is the moral force that resides in society. When this external force, that is, the moral order that controls human appetite for more pleasures or accumulation of goods and services breaks down, people are unable to maintain their psychic equilibrium and related pain and will often solve their psychic discomfort by suicide. We can find similar ideas in Buddhist and Jewish philosophy.

While Durkheim used anomie to explain the variations of suicide rates, anomie can also explain variations in rates of homicide which is the other side of the same coin. Both suicide and homicide are forms of aggression; the first is aggression directed inwardly against oneself, and the latter is directed against others. It therefore follows that the forces that lead to self directed aggression are the selfsame forces that also bring on other-directed aggression.

In this paper I am proposing that the rise of the Holocaust is rooted in a variant of Durkheim's anomie, namely that it was brought on by the fear associated with chaos and legitimated by historical Christian anti-Semitic perspectives.

Faith and Conflict

In Durkheim's view anomie occurs during economic fluctuations and is directly responsible for the rise of suicide rates in a society. Anomie, that is the breakdown in a moral order, occurs both during economic depression and economic growth. It is during such times that life styles which people consider of being their just due changes. He writes: "A genuine regimen exists. Therefore, although not legally formulated, which fixes with relative the maximum degree of ease of living to which each social class may legitimately aspire." (Durkheim, 1951p. 249) In short, people who occupy a certain economic position believe that they have a moral right to their life style. People who enjoy a certain social status believe that they have an intrinsic right to their life style even during an economic depression when their income can no longer support the level of life style to which they became accustomed. In contrast during economic well being when those who previously had little but now when their income has increased feel that they have a legitimate right to have a better life style. The problem, Durkheim proposes, is that as people begin to acquire increased goods and services they have not as yet developed and internalized a moral guide that will define the new limits of their life style. Soon, they their desires exceed their financial ability necessary for maintaining their new desired life style. In this sense a sudden decrease or increase of wealth have this common denominator: they lack an associated moral force that would control peoples desires and permit them to live only to the extent that their incomes permit them. During economic depression people continue to believe to have legitimate rights to their former life and have yet to develop a consciousness of their new social position and accompanying life style. Of course, as a former Talmudic scholar, Durkheim must have been aware of the rhetorical query posed by Ben Zoma: Who is rich? And the answer: he who is satisfied with his given portion. (Talmud "Ethics of Our Fathers" Chapter 4:1) Ben Zoma also said: He who increases wealth also increases worries. Like Ben Zoma, Durkheim also sees that the root unhappiness is associated with economic fluctuations and life style expectations. Both Ben Zoma in first century and Durkheim in the nineteenth century agreed that there is a need for a moral law because only such laws can serve as prophylaxis against the development of insatiable desires.* (Of course Jean Jacque Rousseau similarly advocated that no person can be free unless he first controls his own passions which may also mean their desires.) All these saying and propositions suggest that for a person to have a quality of psychic life he must establish a balance between his desires and the legitimate means by which he can satisfy them. (See also Merton) Durkheim's view of anomie, I believe was influenced by his Jewish education* and also reflects his nineteenth century social perspective which emphasizes that personal stability is an essential part of social order and is more likely to exist in a society that limits social mobility.*

Let me propose that Durkheim's definition of anomie is but one element of a larger social problem namely, the problem of social chaos. I define chaos as the breakdown of people's capability to predict the outcome of their actions. This breakdown can be brought on both by economic and technological changes and to some extent by political upheavals. One paramount consequence associated with social chaos is the destruction of the viability of the culturally defined "if then propositions." When this occurs we are overtaken by fear.

The economic chaos during the Great Depression led, as President Roosevelt indicated in his inaugural speech, to a rise of fear. The fear that people experienced during the depression resulted from the break down of socially defined relationship between action and their consequences. During our socialization we are taught certain truths that are used to guide us in our decision making. For instance, we were taught to believe that hard work and loyalty to employers will assure a steady income and with it a predictable future. What happens when the truths that we have learned and which have guided our lives break down? What happens when people find that the truths that they learned are no longer valid? What happens when our cultural guidelines that we used

Faith and Conflict

to predictors of the future no longer function? The result of such conditions is the rise of fear and as we know, fear leads to frustration and the latter leads to aggression. Suzanne Langer, the noted philosopher pointed out that people can adapt themselves to anything that one can imagine but that people cannot deal with chaos.

Fear generated by chaos is not new. Those who are familiar with the Bible know that according to it God before he could create the world had to bring order out of chaos. Human experience chronicled in history has repeatedly shown that social chaos is highly correlated with fear of an unknown future. However, the intensity of fear leads to an altered and paranoid perception of reality. Paranoid delusion leads to an inability to assess reality. For instance in defeat many people refuse to admit that their country's defeat is the consequence of human action most frequently problems generated by faulty leadership. Instead, they attribute them to all sorts of reasons including God and Fate, that is on conditions outside of their control. Paranoid perspectives, that are often associated with defeat, lead people to blame someone else or some other people for the chaos that they themselves may have caused. Quite frequently they will blame the strangers in their midst. This is the personality trait that Adorno has defined as the authoritarian person, the personality of fascist. (. Adorno et.al.1950)

But paranoia is not necessarily a mental condition that affects individuals it can also affect a society as a whole. It can become a part of a society's culture especially a culture which contains the belief that the believers culture is superior to other societies and their cultures. The result of such paranoid perspective is intolerance to all that is strange and foreign.

In times of social and economic chaos when fear grips a society people will follow leaders who may claim to have immediate solutions to the problems they face who promise to have instant cures for their ills. They seek charismatic leaders who claim that "by virtue [of their relationship with transcendental forces] are set apart from ordinary men and treated as endowed with supernatural, superhuman, or at least specifically exceptional powers or qualities." (Weber, 1947)

Charismatic leaders frequently claim that their power to lead emanates from a divine or at least from a transcendental entity and hence they and they alone have the will, the knowledge, and the relationship with the supernatural to restore order and bring back conditions of status ante quo. Unfortunately under such leadership evil often rises above goodness and justice is subverted by injustice. During chaos induced paranoia truth is either unknown or most likely averted and substituted by falsehood and lies.

Order and chaos are two diametrically opposing conditions. The first is associated with a belief that life in this world is good and the people in it are benevolent. Chaos on the other hand is associated with a belief that the world is unknown and unpredictable and therefore it is to be to be feared. Of course people seek to live in a world that is predictable. We feel safe in such a world that is orderly because we believe that in such a world we have control of the future. We desire a world in which life can be planned and the consequences of our actions can be predicted, a world that is governed by the rationality in the "if - then" propositions.

Human desire to live in a world that can be predicted led early man to believe in the power of the magician. Today in time of chaos the charismatic leader assumes the mantle of the magicians of the past. Of course the development of and the belief in a benevolent God who possesses supreme power has made the belief in magic an anachronism. To solve empirical problems such as health, technology and agriculture and many others we first turn to science. However the extent to which science can save us and solve our problems is limited. When science lacks the necessary knowledge to control the world and solve its problems we turn to faith, to God or to people who claim to have power that they derive from God or any others mystical source. Perhaps the most pervasive problem that science cannot solve is death. I could say

Faith and Conflict

therefore that our fear of death is a fear associated with chaos. Although science may to a great extent secure our life in this world, religion and those claiming to know God argue that they can provide life ever lasting. Our wish for the validity of our "If – then" propositions affect not only our relationship with empirical world based on science but also our life founded in religious beliefs. For instance Christians believe that if one accepts Christ he or she will never die. Judaism, Islam and to some extent Buddhism also provide ways to secure a future life. However, Judaism goes one step further and gives an additional "if then" proposition that affect our lives in this world. For instance, it tells us that "if you shall follow my commandments, then… one will be blessed with well being, but, if you shall not listen to me and will not follow my commandments, then we will suffer negative and undesirable consequences

For the most part all of us plan our lives based on the belief that the future is both predictable and controllable. All of the university students with whom I talked were conditioned early in life and accept the truth of the dictum that if I go to college and if I am successful in achieving required skills then I will get a good paying job and will have a good retirement.

What happens, however, if the propositions that we learned as truth and on which we plan our lives fail us?

There are times in life when reality negates our belief in a predictable world. Many have experienced reversals in our cherished beliefs of a predictable future. How often have we heard about people who spent a great part of their lives in a job for which they were well prepared and which they believed would be their life's career only to have their expectations of a career destroyed. Most adults have in one way or another experienced that advances in technology makes their knowledge obsolete. What about the myriads of people who put their trust in the stock market as their response to the adage a penny saved is a penny earned only to find that the cultural advice failed them? There were millions, for instance, who believed in the predictable success of Enron and in the end lost their savings and with it the quality life that they believed would be their future? Such are chaotic conditions shake our trust not only in society but also in our ability to assure a good future for ourselves. Such were the conditions in Germany after World War I. In this country the events of 9/11 have also had a great effect on our belief of American security and many of us today are fearful because we our perception of the future is chaotic and we see it as unpredictable.

My father told me stories how the breakdown of the "if – then" proposition brought on by inflation in Germany during the 1920s led to loss of faith in their own capability to control their fate and have faith in a predictable outcome of actions. One such story is about two brothers who lived during the 1920's hyper-inflation in Germany. These two brothers had diametrically opposing personalities and social values. The older brother was a hard working person who believed in the nineteenth century capitalist rationality that hard work and investments will assure him a good future. He had total faith in the efficacy of industriousness and in investments. Each month he took a portion of his earnings and earmarked it for investment. The younger brother hated work. He was a bon vivant who loved to drink and to have a good time without a concern for the future. When their father died each brother inherited a share of their father's wealth. The older one immediately took it and invested it in a traditional way while the younger brother used his legacy to create a well stocked wine cellar. After World War I when Germany suffered major economic setbacks and extreme hyper-inflation the older brother lost all his investments while he younger brother's wine cellar together with his empty bottles made him far richer than his older brother.

People's response to the fear generated by a state of chaos is to seek a way to re-establish status quo ante to bring back the "good old days." They believe that their pain and fear can be alleviated by re-establishing the conditions that existed before the chaos ensued. They

Faith and Conflict

seek a revolutionary change – that is, they seek a radical and immediate alteration of conditions that will re-establish the previous social order. In short they seek a magician who can perform this miracle. To achieve such retrogressive changes Germans have gladly give up reason and followed a charismatic leader who promises that he has the will, the power, and the charisma to bring immediate remedies and bring back the "good ole days." There is however a price that must be paid for the promised magic by the charismatic leaders.

The price starts with the charismatic leader's demand to suspend rationality and place their faith in the efficacy of the leader similar to the faith they placed in religion and its leaders. Charismatic leaders, similar to religious leaders, demand unquestioned loyalty, obedience, and faith in and commitment to their teaching (Max Weber, 1947). Charismatic leaders, like religious leaders, teach that the world is in a continual struggle between us and them the believers and unbelievers. They propose that world is bifurcated it is either black or white; there is no neutrality and there are no gray areas. The faith that religion demands in name of God is similar those demanded by charismatic leaders in the name of his god – the cause. He, like religious leaders demands complete and total submission to his point of view. Both religious and charismatic leaders are intolerant of other points of views and neither accepts the possibility that there exists goodness and truth outside of their teaching. (See Feuerbach). Such faith because of its rigidity, divides the world into "we and they." With this dichotomy the leader defines "others" as being dangerous to the well being of the state and declares them to be the root cause of all problems of all economic or social ills. Such a point of view enhances the division between us and them and serves both as rationale and legitimacy for developing a hostile attitude against the others – the "strangers" in society.

If a charismatic leader's advocacy for aggression towards the others, the outsiders, the non-believers if it is to be accepted must rooted in and legitimated by existing cultural beliefs. The charismatic leader does not necessarily provide a new perspective of the strangers he merely reinforces existing beliefs and views. For instance Hitler's hostility toward Jews was not a new ideology. Anti-Semitism it has a long history in Germany and strong roots in Luther's teaching.

For the charismatic leader to be successful in advocating hostilities toward strangers the following a- priory conditions need to exist. First, the legitimacy of aggression toward "others" is based on a priori cultural perspectives that labels minority groups as "institutionalized strangers." Next, there need also to exist values that advocate the infallibility of the majority's culture. Third, there also needs to be present a culturally approved value system that advocates the idea that the stranger is a threat not only to the nation's existence but also to its sanctity. And finally there needs to exist in the majority's cultural system stereotypical description of the stranger as the evil incarnate who desecrates the purity of the majority, in short, there needs to exist culturally supported teachings that demonizes the stranger.

Faith and Conflict

The Institutionalized Strangers:

Who are these institutionalized strangers that are perceived as a threat to society? The term stranger, as a general rule, refers to foreigners, intruders, and impermanent residents and wonderers. They are people whose culture, values, language, and often religion differ from the majority in a society and because of these differences they are perceived to be dangerous to society. But as Georg Simmel proposes, strangers in a community are not wanderers. To the contrary, they are people who came and stayed. Strangers are permanent residents, minority groups whose ethnicity and hence culture differs in some manner from the majority. Very frequently the strangers have for centuries been permanent residents of a community or a state. Yet, in spite of their long existence in the community, the stranger is non-the-less always perceived by the majority to be a separate entity and never an integral part of the community both socially and physically. Strangers are often defined as a necessary evil. They are necessary to the economy but are socially undesirable.

In this sense strangers are given a tenuous and temporary status – they are institutionalized – and are reluctantly tolerated. As a general rule, strangers are permitted to reside both physically and socially in the periphery of the community. They are tolerated only because they perform necessary tasks that members of the majority are forbidden to carry out either by custom or by religion and because the remuneration for such services is low and inadequate to provide the life style and corresponding status enjoyed by the majority. Jews in the Christian world were, for example, were permitted to stay only if they become bankers, a task that Christian laws of usury forbade the faithful to perform. For instance, in 1182 Philip August king of France after having despoiled and imprisoned the Jews of France ordered their expulsion. But, for financial reasons in 1198 the same Philip Augustus recalled the Jews made them serfs to the king and charged them to provide banking services. Quite frequently Jews were forbidden by law to become active in occupations that were defined as honorable. An edict by the Council of Orleans in 539 prohibited Christians from having any sort of social intercourse with Jews. They were also were prohibited to eat with and marry Jews. In the feudal societies the nobility and the guilds forbade Jews from owning land and engage in agriculture or in the crafts. Further separation of Jews from the population has been enhanced with the introduction of various calumnies such as blood accusation, that is, the belief that Jews need the blood of Christian children to bake Matza the bread that Jews use for Passover. The persecution of Jews became the order of the era. In Egypt during the early Pharaohs, the tasks considered as unclean such as the embalming and all tasks associated with burials were assigned to strangers.

In central Europe in my own time (1925-44) Gypsies cleaned and disposed the accumulated waste in outhouses. Like Jews, they too, lived apart from the community and like Jews who lived in Jewish neighborhoods such as the Juderias in Spain and Portugal and in Juden Gasses (Jewish streets) in Germany and Central Europe, Gypsies too lived separately in assigned areas. In Munkacs, the city of my birth, there was the "Cigany utca" the Gypsy Street as well as the "Yiddische Gas" the Jewish Street. Both streets were considered to be lower class neighborhood a street where the poorest Gypsies and the poorest Jews lived. None the less it was a pleasant experience to walk in the Gypsy street during the warm summer days for there the sound of music and the pleasant fragrance of the lilac trees permeated the neighborhoods. In the United States prior to the Civil Rights Act, there was a clear demarcation between what was considered to be white and black labor.

There were times, however, when the outsiders would intrude as supernumeraries and occupy economic positions once held by members

Faith and Conflict

of the majority. When strangers leave their assigned tasks and intrude on work that traditionally were allocated to the members of the community, when they seek higher social positions then, they are accused as usurping the true inhabitant's natural rights. These economic rights that were allocated strictly to members of the dominant ethnic group were legitimated by the dominant religion namely, declaring that that these rights to certain occupations and land ownership were granted to them by God. The idea that God assigned a particular land to a people has a long history perhaps even older than the rights of the Jews to Israel as described in the Bible. Under these conditions, the greater the numbers of the stranger who have transgressed against caste-like social and economic positions the stronger becomes the perception that they are a threat to the community. Still the community in most instances did not become hostile to the strangers, even when they become supernumerary. Hostilities toward strangers most often occurred as a result of a decline in the community's economic conditions when the ruling majority feared for their future and their economic security.

Cultural infallibility:

Even when the community perceived the strangers as a threat they would not respond aggressively against them unless the following conditions were also present. First, of course, there needed to be a charismatic leader who would direct the community's attention to the strangers as the cause of the social chaos and ensuing problems. Second, the community must to support the charismatic leader's claim that the strangers are dangerous people akin to demons or as anti-Christ and finally, the majority must believe in the infallibility and the sanctity of their culture.

Cultural beliefs, values, and religion have one common feature they are perceived by members of society as being true, right, and above all else as flawless. Consequently any criticism of the majority's cultural beliefs assumes the character of being disrespectful of the sanctity of the belief system and hence disloyal to the society. For instance, when I arrived to the United States I soon learned that I cannot be critical of the American values and of the American way of life. People always asked, as I am sure they ask most new immigrants: What do you think of the United States? As long as my response was positive, people listened to me even though impatiently. However, I if I dared to make a critical comment I was chastised: "Well! If you don't like it here why don't you go back where you came from!" Moreover, culture, that is values and beliefs of a society even when they are secular beliefs are also endowed with an element of sanctity. Most people accept the culture's sanctity, namely that their shared beliefs, social values and the country's life style are transcendental to the individual that is, they are greater and more important than the individual. Jean Jacque Rousseau was the first to recognize the existence of the existence of a faith that is founded on and arises out of one's civic association and belief in one's country. This sacred belief rooted in civic association he called "Civil Religion."

Faith and Conflict

He writes in his book The Social Contract: The dogmas of civil religion ought to be simple in numbers, precisely fixed, and without explanation and comment. [These dogmas include] the existence of a powerful, wise and benevolent Divinity, who foresees and provides the life to come, the happiness of the just, the punishment of the wicked, the sanctity of the social contract and laws; these are its positive dogmas. It's negative dogmas I would confine to intolerance.(Quoted in Bellah 1980 p.27)

The problem is that most civil religions, like church religions, and unlike what Rousseau proposed, do not advocate universalism. In most societies civil religion and church religion are merged and become dogmatic just like church based religious beliefs. The sanctity of the civil religion is rooted in the society's history, their ancestors, and to a perception of a god who has a particularistic relationship with the nation. All of these features infuse the members of the community or society with the belief that their culture i.e., that their beliefs and world view, cannot be erroneous. While all societies have such a commitment to their culture they also differ in the degree to which they stress the element of cultural infallibility. By this I mean that cultures differ in the degree to which they propose that their society, their value system, their moral, and religious beliefs are true and correct while others are faulty. Symbols of cultural infallibility are contained in such expressions as "God is an Englishman", even in the statement "America – love it or leave it" or as the German military belt buckles declared "Got mit uns" (God is with us). Similarly all nations treat their national anthem as though it were a religious hymn and their flags as a sacred symbol. Of course cultural infallibility is rooted in the notion of being chosen by God and therefore the nation and its culture stands above all other nations. The sanctity of cultural infallibility as an ideology is expressed in a society's civil religion that proposes a belief that they are selected by the deity for special treatment and hence they perceive their society to be always right, unspoiled, and sacred. Bellah quotes

Cultural infallibility:

Hans Kohn that people in the United States perceive this country to be the American Israel to the extent that some believe that God has made a new covenant with the U.S. like in earlier times he made with Israel. This special relationship with God is central to our belief in our manifest destiny. But the U.S. is not the only country that has such perspectives. The Nazi ideology proposed that nature has endowed them with superior qualities which justified their various conquests. To keep from being alienated from God or from any other transcendental figure or power that endows the country with superior status the nation must be true to its mission since it is believed to be defined by the transcendent. In this way societies assume the mantle of holiness. This was not very much unlike the XIX century American belief in the principle of manifest destiny. This term combined a near-religious belief in America's right for expansionism, including the belief in American exeptionalism and nationalism coupled with a belief in the natural superiority of what was then called the "Anglo-Saxon race" referring to white Americans and Britons.

Most charismatic leaders, during times of national stress, often use Biblical metaphors to explain the reason for the rise of problems. The explanations used for national problems are very similar to those found in the Old Testament. Like the Jewish view of their relationship with God, other countries, including the United States, propose that when a holy society lusts for strange ideas and incorporates elements of other peoples' cultures into its own then the nation loses its authenticity and as a punishment there is the rise of chaos and economic and moral decay. It is in such times when charismatic leaders assume the role of the prophet and demand that the country return to its true and sacred way of life one that is void of foreign contamination. The stronger a society's belief is in their culture's infallibility, the more likely then will be that when social chaos arises the charismatic prophet will demand that the nation cleanse itself of foreign influences and return to its original national purity. Often such acts of cleansing include the need for

Faith and Conflict

the destruction of the strangers who now are seen as the cause of the society's problems.

At such time the perspectives of the secular "civil religion" and the dominant religion will unite and claim proprietorship over the society's moral and ethical values. For instance in Western societies at such times secular morals will give way to Christian morals and a person who lives a moral life will be defined not only as a good person but most importantly as a Christian gentleman. In this sense Christianity and Islam and Orthodox Judaism usurp moral proprietorship. In Germany the Nazi value system that in a way has become a quasi religious system that has influenced the religious teachings and both advocated the importance of national purity that was defined as racial purity. Only by adhering to the ideas of Aryan purity will, the German people were assured, Germany's physical prowess and success in dominating others nation return.

Toward the end of World War II the American Jewish Committee engaged Max Horkheimer a former member of the Institute of Social research in Frankfurt Germany to investigate the causes of anti-Semitism. Horkheimer together with Adorno, Erich Fromm, and Nevitt Sanford sought to determine how personality structure influenced to anti-Semitism and racism.

One of their significant finding was that those who are anti-Semitic and racist tend to be submissive to and be uncritical of authority figures. (Adorno et.al. 1950) The tendency to be submissive to authority figures, I propose was a part of the German culture and is a remnant of the German caste structure that was dominant till the end of World War II. No wonder that Hitler was looked upon as "Der Fuhrer" the leader. Perhaps the best indication of authoritarian submission is the acceptance of the dictum: The Fuhrer commands and we follow. German authoritarianism, at least the propensity to be submissive to authority figures, I suggest have its roots in the German feudal culture.

Cultural infallibility:

The German tendency for authoritarian submission was quite evident in 1946 when I escaped from Czechoslovakia and returned to Germany. After my liberation from German concentration camp I came to Prague to pursue my childhood dream to study medicine. Soon it became evident that the Czechoslovakia that I knew and loved the one that existed pre 1938 is disappearing. The freedoms that were a central feature of that country when Massaryk and Benes were the prime ministers were being substituted by communist authoritarianism. I and three of my high school friends, all survivors of camps, decided to escape. The Jewish Federation in Prague offered to help us escape if we were to take with us about a dozen or so pre-teen Jewish orphaned boys who were survivors of German camps. Two days later with the help of a guide we the boys and I with my class mate Chayim Sternbach crossed the Czech border into Germany. We had to wait till morning for a train that would take us to Munich and to the Funk Kasserne, a former military barracks that now served as housing of Displaced Persons (DP's). By morning the boys became hungry. I had neither money nor food-coupons with which to purchase food. Chayim Sternbach and I devised a plan to secure food. Since I had a better command of English I would impersonate an American counter-intelligence officer and Chayim will be my interpreter. I had my student tram card with my picture and numerous official stamps that gave the appearance of an important ID. Equipped with this ID we entered a bakery I flashed it and claimed to be a member of the Army Intelligence in civic and with a strong commanding voice I requisitioned five loaves of bread. Chayim translated my English. Without hesitation they handed me the requested bread. Using the same technique I was successful in obtaining various sausages from the butcher. Were they not to have been were socialized into a culture emphasizing submissiveness to authority I would have been challenged particularly if for nothing because of my youth (I was nineteen) and would have not gotten the food that was badly needed by the boys – as well as by me.

Faith and Conflict

Demonization:

When societies become aggressive against minorities, that is, against institutionalized strangers, they justify and legitimate their action with negative stereotypical definitions of the strangers. These descriptions are a part of the majority's xenophobic culture that defines the strangers both as individuals and as collectives as dangerous people because they are seeking to usurp the majority's rights and their political power. By religion they are defined as demons, anti-Christ and secularly as historical enemies. In Europe, the demonization of Jews was based on the New Testament's description of them as persons who are damned by God, and who are eternally guilty for having committed deicide. They are depicted not only as evil bankers, money lenders, and usurers but who also as dangerous people who because their faiths demands that they use Christian blood for Passover. These descriptions were annually reinforced through sermons and passion-plays. (Gibson's movie The Passion of the Christ is a modern version of the passion play and is very similar both in content and form to those performed for centuries in Oberammergau.) The Holocaust, for instance, would not have occurred, argues James Carroll, were it not for the way the Church from its incipiency demonized the Jews. The attribution of negative characters based on beliefs and on misinterpreted history is an essential feature in justification system of a people's participation in the Holocaust.

In the long history of demonizing strangers, aggression against them is often legitimated as a religious act of cleansing. After all, strangers not only have a different culture but most importantly have a different religion and aggression against them is being legitimated as a necessary act of national purification. We encounter the act of demonizing in the Book of Esther in the Bible. Haman the villain in the story proposes to king Ahasaerus the following: "There is a certain people scattered abroad and dispersed among the peoples in all the provinces of thy kingdom; and their laws are diverse from those of every people; neither keep they the king's laws; therefore it profits not the king to suffer them. If it pleases the king, let it be written that they be destroyed." (Bible, Esther 3:8) Demonizing is one method used by the allies during World War II depicting both Hitler and especially the Japanese as villains not to be trusted – they are "evil" incarnate. Today we find that in the struggle that has pitted the United States against some Islamic States we tend to demonize our enemies and in turn they demonize us. We often pervert history and use it to demonize our enemies. We all remember the slogan "Remember the Alamo" an admonition designed to maintain a negative attitude against another ethnic group or nation. Such injunctions to remember are resplendent in the Bible. Jews are taught to remember their history with Egypt and especially with the Amalekites and Moabites. In fact Jews were commanded to erase the memory of Amalek from under the sky. Perhaps most nations and tribes in this world have such historical memories. The Christian Bible, at least in my view perverts history and demonizes Jews by depicting the Pharisees as the evil persons whose attitudes toward Christ had direct bearing on his death. Therefore the Jews because of their rejection of Christ are damned by God. Early wars that split Islam into Shiites and Sunnis are still remembered and are sources for cross demonization. The struggle against the conquests of the Ottoman Empire is one reason for hostilities that led to genocide and the breakup of the former Yugoslavia.

In that country ethnic groups were pitted against each other. Each ethnic group using their historical memory coupled with religious differences justify their acts of aggression. I am sure that similar ethnic memories are used to justify and genocides in Africa.

I have outlined a brief theoretical explanation for the rise of the Holocaust. As a survivor of the Holocaust I am looking for ways that would help to diminish the hostile reactions among people when facing chaos. No social system can eliminate social changes and economic

Faith and Conflict

variations that are caused by man or nature. We can however, make people aware that our fears generated by social and economic chaos were used to legitimate our anger and hostilities towards minorities. Reactions against Jews which led to the Holocaust were supported by existing ideologies that demonized Jews. We still read Shakespeare's depiction of Shylock. Ferdinand Marian's Jud Suss and Karl Marx's diatribe titled "On the Jewish Question. James Carroll in his recent book points out that the perspectives that led to the Holocaust and to the destruction of six million Jews is rooted in the Christian teachings and in the Biblical description of Jews. He suggests that it is time that the Church (and let me add – all Christianity) need to repent their sins that were committed against Jews. The few apologies that the Catholic Church offered to Jews is merely perfunctory "mea culpa." Carroll comments these apologies never constituted "authentic repentance." Instead "apologies [are] offered too glibly, in other words, [that] can be a sly way of asserting one's own moral superiority while reifying the victim status of the group to whom apologies are offered." (Carroll 2001, 599-600)Hostilities against Jews were also introduced into Protestantism by Martin Luther in his book "Jews and Their Lies."

How can we alter and change inter-religious and inter-ethnic hostilities? It cannot be other than the re-interpretation of the Biblical description of Jesus' death. Jews must be totally cleared from the two millennia old accusation of deicide. Christians of all denominations must introduce into their theology a strong and genuine effort to eliminate the historic forms of demonizing Jews by eliminating the passion plays which have served to create anti-Jewish attitudes. Moreover Christianity must bring forth new and benign meanings in the stories of Christ's death.

The teaching of the psychology, sociology, and history of genocides must be made a part of public and private school curriculum. We must make all students aware that no nation and no society can be immune to chaos and react with hatred to minorities. If we fail to educate the

Demonization:

public of what we are capable, we merely continue to justify hostile reactions. We the people of the United States are not immune to the forces and conditions that led other nations to create holocausts of all kinds. We too can become hostile to strangers and develop paranoid perceptions of them. This is evident in our reaction to 9/11. Let us not forget the mass internment of U.S. citizens of Japanese extraction during World War II. In short no one should see the splinter in other people's eyes before they see the log in their own.

If we the United States seeks to become a true world leader we must achieve it not by power alone. We the people of the United States must first and foremost become a nation in which justice prevails. We must find ways by which we assure all people of an equal chance for a peaceful and healthy life.

Notes

* Durkheim's father was a rabbi. In fact, his family history shows and he stems from a rabbinical dynasty of seven generations of rabbis. His early education was immersed in Jewish education in the anticipation that he too will follow his father's footsteps and become a rabbi.

References:

T.W. Adorno, Else Frenkeel-Brunswick, J. Levinson, and R. N. Sanford. The Authoritarian Personality (New York, Harper, 1950) Bellah, Robert and P.E.Hammond 1980 Varieties of Civil Religion

Faith and Conflict

Harper and Row. Bible, The Book of Esther Carroll, James 2001, Constantine's Sword: The Church and the Jews, Boston Houghton Mifflin Co.

Durkhein, Emile 1951 Suicide trans. J.A. Spaulding and GT. Simpson New York. The Free Press

Feuerbach, Ludwig 1957. The Essence of Christianity (Trans. George Eliot) N.Y. Harper Torch Book

Langer, Suzanne (1942) Philosophy in a New Key: A study in the symbolism of reason, rite, and art. New York: McMillan and Co.

Malinowski, Bronislaw, 1992, Magic, Science, and Religion Waveland Press

Merton, Robert K. 1968, Social Theory and Social Structure Glencoe Ill. The Free Press.

Simmel, Georg 1950, The Sociology of Georg Simmel trns. Kurt

H. Wolff. The Free Press of Glencoe Ill. Max Weber 1947 The Theory of Social and Economic Organization A.M Henderson and T. Parsons trans. Glencoe Ill. The Free Press. 68

Section III: Christian Jewish Dialectic

Preface to section III

As a young boy I was cautioned by my maternal grandparents who lived in a very small village in the Carpathian Mountains not to be seen on the village street during Easter. It was during Easter that the priests and ministers spoke of Jesus' death and of course of the Jewish complicity in the deicide. In the last two millennia Jews have experienced various hostile act associated with the Easter season. One common accusation of that period was that Jews used Christian blood to bake the unleavened bread, the matzah. Why have the Christians maintained a historic hostility against Jews? I propose to examine this question in the next two essays.

From its incipiency Christianity sought to separate and diverge itself from Judaism the faith that contain its roots? A simple and direct answer is: The leaders of this new religion sought to give Christianity an identity of its own. To accomplish this task, like any other ideology, it became the anti-thesis to Judaism the original thesis. Christianity now has become the anti-thesis in its dialectical relationship with Judaism. And, like in any dialectical relationship those reflecting an antithetical point of view not only are they opposed to the ideals of the old thesis but the members of the new group those in developing

Faith and Conflict

a negative perspective advocated by the old class (in this instance religion) also developed a hostile attitude toward them – the Jews. In this sense Christianity not only became different from Judaism but looked at Judaism and Jews as its hostile competitor.

Judaism and the Jews have thus become an object of distrust and of hatred. In the Christian view Jews not only have lost their special relationship with God but also have lost their chance for grace and salvation. Christianity has set forth a new direction one where people could substitute the Jewish view accountability as the sine qua non for salvation with love and faith in Christ. Christians no longer were held responsible for their hostile treatment of non Christians especially of Jews who reject their theology.

The essays in this section contain my analysis of the bifurcation of the Christian and Jewish values of love and justice. I attempt to show how love particularly in the Reformation period has led to individualism and a concern for rights without necessarily the associated duties. Based on this analysis, I propose that the term "Judeo-Christian values" do not reflect reality of the deep separation of values that have occurred in the last two millennia.

Isaac and Jesus: The Two Sacrifices In Christian – Jewish Dialectic

One of the great convergences in Jewish and Christian legends revolves around the birth, the life and the sacrifice of Jesus and Isaac. In this essay, I wish to examine these similarities that have become important to Christian theologians. The two most significant similarities revolve around the foretelling of their births and God's ordination that both should be sacrificed. For instance both Isaac's and Jesus' births were foretold by angels to their parents. The second important similarity is Isaac's binding, that is, the ordination of Isaac's sacrifice, and of course Jesus' death as a sacrifice on the cross. Unlike orthodox theologians, both Jewish and Christian, who take their respective biblical stories as God revealed truth my concern, as a social scientist, was to propose more rational explanation of this duplicity. What intrigued me was why early Christians chose to retell the Isaac story and substituting Jesus as the new protagonist and minimizing, in fact eliminating the other stories related with Abraham. It is my intention to examine and compare the Isaac and Jesus legends from a socio-historical point of view rather than from a traditional theological perspective and thereby I hope to add to our understanding for the two millennia old Christian hostility to Jews.

Faith and Conflict

Even a cursory examination of Christian theological literature shows the existence of a plethora of theological explanations for similarities between these two legends. The common denominator in the Christian theological explanation is the belief that Isaac was a prophetic representation of the coming of Jesus who would introduce a new religion that would supersede traditional Judaism. This idea, for instance, is central in the articles published by the Christian Apologetics & Research Ministry. But, a more rational explanation is one that is consistent with the views espoused in the Christian Bible that the new story lays the foundation for a Christian dialectic against Judaism. The retelling of the Isaac story is used to legitimate the supremacy of Christianity over historical Judaism.

In Christian theology both Jesus' birth and his death as a God ordained sacrifice is central to Christianity's raison d'être. In Judaism the central figure in the sacrifice story that is, the akeydah (his binding for the sacrifice) is Abraham. The akeydah is merely one of the two important stories in the Abraham saga. The central figure in Genesis 22 is not Isaac but Abraham. Isaac's birth, the akeydah, and Abraham's confrontation with God in the story of Sodom and Gomorrah are the vehicles by which Abraham declares the two foundations of the Jewish religion: faith and morals. The story of Isaac reflects the Jewish emphasis on the importance of faith that is the belief in God's existence as well as our trust in God's munificence as it is described in Psalm 27. The second significant belief in Judaism's, one that is not given strong emphasis in Christianity, is contained in the Sodom and Gomorrah story. The akeydah and Sodom and Gomorrah are in Judaism intrinsically interrelated. In the Sodom story God emphasizes the importance of both individual and collective morality. The essence of the Sodom and Gomorrah story, from the Jewish perspective, is that that both individuals and societies are accountable for their moral lives.

Isaac and Jesus: The Two Sacrifices In Christian – Jewish Dialectic

In this chapter I am proposing the following thesis : Christianity by giving precedence to the sacrificial elements in the Isaac–Jesus stories and minimizing and eliminating the Sodom Gomorrah story Abraham and the religious revolution:

has placed primacy on faith and minimized God's demand on morals. What is most important to me is that Christianity by devaluing Biblical moral issues and with it also minimizing human accountability for moral adherence as necessary for salvation. Instead Christianity for reasons that I am describing in a latter essay chose to emphasize love, forgiveness, and salvation through faith alone. In short, I am proposing that the Christian stress on the individual and the minimization of the believer's accountability for his behavior as well as by placing primacy on faith and with it on the ease of forgiveness through Jesus has made hostilities against Jews easy and thereby contributed to a belief system that indirectly led to the existence of the Holocaust.

Such a relationship has already been suggested by Garry Wills in his introduction to G. Passelecq and Sucheckey (1997) tome The Papal Sin (2000). Similarly and even with greater stress Carroll (2001) proposes that the Catholic theology of the last two millennia had an enormous impact on the rise of Christian hostilities against Jews culminating with the Holocaust. The hostility against Jews that began by the Catholic Church during the rule of Constantine did not end with the Reformation. Per contra Luther while disagreeing with the Catholic Church on many issues has retained Christian faith based hostilities against Jews and in his noted essay "Jews and Their Lies " he reinforces the legitimacy anti-Jews edicts issued by Constantine the Great in 350 CE.

Faith and Conflict

Abraham and the religious revolution:

The best way to start the comparison of Isaac and Jesus is to begin with a few biographical notes of Abraham's life. After all, from my point of view, Abraham and not Isaac is the central figure in the story of the akeydah. Abraham was born in the city of Ur in Chaldea in the land between the Tigress and the Euphrates. As an adult, he moved to Haran a great Sumerian city. Both the Chaldean and Sumerian religions into which Abraham was born and into which he was socialized by his father Terah, a priest in the Sumerian religion, included the rites of human sacrifice. These sacrifices were common among the Middle Eastern religions. For instance the Bible cautions Jews that anyone found worshipping Molech, the God who demanded the sacrifice of children, will be punished by death.

The Abraham saga begins from the time that he was commanded by God to leave his native land and travel to the place that "I'll show you." Abraham, a man of faith, left his father's house and took his extended family west-ward towards the Mediterranean Sea to the land of the Canaan.

In the Bible Abraham is presented to us as a revolutionary protagonist for the idea of monotheism. In the Biblical stories Abraham seeks to give us a glimpse of a new view of God. Abraham enters the scene of history by proclaiming a new and revolutionary idea of monotheism, the belief in one invisible God who is concerned with morality rather than cultism, who not only controls the world but who is also a moral arbiter in human and social life. This new god is not only the creator of the world but is also a judge of people's behavior. Unlike earlier views of God who are tyrannical this new God himself is bound by the same moral principles that He demands from humans. This new God is just

Isaac and Jesus: The Two Sacrifices In Christian – Jewish Dialectic

and merciful. He is a judge guided by one prime principle – the moral dictum of justice. He differs from the old gods because Adonai (the master) places precedence on moral behavior rather than cultic rituals. Unlike the Canaanite gods, this new invisible god is neither blood thirsty nor is he merciless. (Of course, because He is still in a developmental stage sometimes he reverts to harshness.) Abraham's god unlike

Molech cannot be appeased by the sacrifice of human blood although he does accept the blood and flesh of animals. Abraham's God defines human blood as sacred because it is the symbol of life and therefore its shedding is a fundamental wrong.

Abraham's description of this new God is an evolutionary step toward a universal religion. This new view of God redefines man's relationship both with Him and with his fellow man. In this sense Abraham is the forerunner of Isaiah's view of God. Isaiah took the next important step in the evolution of religion by minimizing, if not eliminating, the importance of cult altogether. Most importantly, Abraham presents us with a first glimpse of a universal god, one that is bound neither to a specified territory nor to a particular society.

Throughout the Bible there are stories in which God seeks to test people's faith in Him. The writers of the scritures have devoted one whole book the book – the allegorical story of Job depicting such a test. Job is the universal man – he is not a Jew. The book of Job seeks to teach us the following" first the essentiality of morality, second that human being are being judged on their morality and finally the essence of faith in a God whose action is most often incomprehensible to man.

Like God who tested Job, God similarly seeks to tests Abraham's faith. God comes to Abraham and commands him to take Isaac, his only son whom he loves, to the Land of Moriah and offer him as a sacrifice to Him. Of course Abraham follows God's wishes. He comes to the appointed place, builds an altar and sets his son on top of the wood which will provide the fire for a burnt offering. Just as Abraham is about to use his knife to kill Isaac, an angel sent by God, holds his

Faith and Conflict

arm and tells him:" Do not lay your hand on the boy, and do nothing to him; for I know now that (you?) revere God, seeing that you have not refused your son, your only son." Abraham sees the ram that God ordained and substitutes it for his son. God then reiterates his covenant with Abraham*.

There are two essential elements in this story. First, of course, is the declaration of the essentiality of faith and the second is God's rejection of human sacrifice.

Let us now look at the similarities between Isaac's binding and the story of Jesus' sacrifice for which he is known as "the lamb" quite similar to the ram. Christian Apologetics and Research Ministry's publication cites sixteen points of similarities between the Isaac story and Jesus' birth and death. In this paper I shall but look at some of the more significant similarities. The first similarity is the announcement of their births. When Abraham was ninety God appears as "El Shaddai" and tells him (and I assume that the communication was in a dream,) that Sarah will bear a child whose progeny will be the rulers of people. Similarly we are also told of the appearance of the angels who reiterated God's promise to Abraham when announcing to him the birth of his son. We find a similar story regarding the foretelling of the birth of Jesus. In the Gospel of St. Mathew, we are told that an angel of God appeared to Joseph in a dream and foretold the birth of Jesus who should be named Jesus for he shall save the world from the consequences of their sins.

The Christian Bible tells us that God sends His son his only begotten son, his beloved son, to earth where he shall be sacrificed.. Similarly God tells Abraham: Take now your son, your only son, whom you love, Isaac, and take him into the Land of Moriah; and offer him there for a burnt- offering on one of the mountains that will tell you. In the Christian Bible Abraham the father of Isaac is substituted by God the father of Jesus who, we are told, "so loved the world, that he gave his only begotten Son, (John 3:16). Not only was Jesus God's only son but according to Mark, God spoke out of a cloud to Jesus' disciples informing them that Jesus is his beloved son (Mark 9:7). So both Isaac and Jesus are described with the same adjectives: they are their father's only and beloved son to be offered as a sacrifice. In the case of Isaac we know that God ordained Abraham to sacrifice his son as a test of his faith. But is this not so with Jesus: after all Christian theology claims that Jesus is God's son. Why then did God ordain Jesus to be sacrificed? Of course – it is God his father who wants Jesus' death. Jesus reaffirms this when on the cross he states "Thy will be done." But for what purpose does God send his son Jesus to earth so that he later is to be sacrificed? Unlike Isaac, Jesus' faith is not being tested. Jesus is offered as atonement for the world's sins, more specifically, for Adam's sin. Thus God does not ask for the individual's atonement; Jesus' atones for the collective sin one that is passed by birth – the original sin. In this sense Jesus is indeed the sacrificial lamb, perhaps more like the escape-goat that the High Priest has offered in the Temple on the Day of Atonement to atone for the Jews personal and collective sins. God, in the Christian view, seeks to sacrifice his only begotten son to atone for past, present and future sins of humanity.

When Jews offered sacrifices to God, they did so as a means to appease God's anger and to gain his favor. Is Jesus being sacrificed for the same reason? But herein lays the issue of irrationality. It is one thing for people to think that they must appease the power that controls their life. But why does God need to appease himself? Why, at least from the Christian point of view, must God sacrifice not an animal but a super human being – God's only son? God proclaims that Jesus' be sacrificed as atonement for the "original sin." Jesus is pre-ordained to give his life as atonement for Adam and Eve. Christianity proposes that Jesus' death will lift the eternal punishment imposed by Adam's sin that of the loss of Paradise. That is, through Jesus people can regain eternal life in Paradise that Adam and Eve have lost. Unlike Jewish conception of sacrifice that is an act of free will it is not so with Jesus.

Faith and Conflict

Jesus' death was preordained by what is seemingly a harsher God than the one depicted in the Jewish Bible.

Thus these two stories points to the great differences between the Jewish view of God and the Christian view. First, Abraham had a choice. He could reject God's demand, but Jesus doesn't have a choice. Next, God ordains the appearance of a ram so that human blood will not be shed. But this is not so with regard to Jesus. God demands his own appeasement through his son's sacrifice. Does this not depict God as a non-loving, merciless, and vindictive entity who must have his "pound of flesh?" Does not this view belie the Christian claim that God is pure love? There must be another reason for inconsistency in Christian theology. There must be another reason why Christianity has this harsher image of God who must sacrifice his only begotten son a reason that is not consonant with and the claim that God is pure love. The answer we are told that God sacrifices Jesus out of love of humanity. This is achieved by declaring that Jesus' sacrifice is God's gift to humanity. According to Christian belief, Jesus' life was the gift that God gave to mankind through which they now have the means for salvation. " The Christian Bible tells that Christ, like Isaac, willingly laid down his life for the sake of humanity. In essence this is a double gift one given by God and Jesus his son. Of course this is not a gift to all humanity but only for those who accept with utmost faith the belief that Jesus was (and is) the son of God. (John 3:16) Specifically, John tells us (4:9) that God so loved us that He "sent his only begotten son into the world that we might live through him." Peter (1:9) states the consequence of faith in Jesus is the salvation of one's soul. In Ephesians Paul emphasizes that "by grace are you saved through faith; and that not of yourselves: it is the gift of God." In short, no one needs to be accountable for his or her deeds. Forgiveness is guaranteed through faith and faith alone. This is especially true in Luther's theology. Still, I must wonder couldn't have God appeased himself without having to sacrifice his Son?

Isaac and Jesus: The Two Sacrifices In Christian – Jewish Dialectic

The similarity of these two sacrifice tales indicates, at least to me, that Christianity from its incipience formed a dialectical relationship with Judaism. Christianity became the anti-thesis to the Jewish thesis. The first element of belief that Christianity seeks to negate is the belief that Jews continue to have a covenant with God one that was forged through Abraham. After all, if God's covenant with Jews is still valid, then Christians cannot but have a lesser relationship with God. If Christianity wished to change this idea and to emphasize instead that they are more beloved by God it had to destroy the legitimacy of the Jewish claim of being the am segulah – God's chosen and beloved people. Christianity did so by declaring that Christianity has through Jesus' sacrifice superseded the old covenant that is associated with a ram by a superior sacrifice of God's son and thereby indicating and that now they are God's chosen people.

Thus the dialectic has been set. On the one hand stands the old thesis that the covenant God made with Abraham and his descendants who have inherited this covenant which will make them God's chosen people with all its benefits. This is reaffirmed by Isaac when he blessed Jacob that nations will bow down and serve his seed. When a Jewish boy is circumcised, the father recites the blessing that tells that he, the father, is fulfilling his obligation to introduce the son into the covenant of Abraham. At that ceremony we proclaim "in blood you shall live". And with it Jews are continually assured that all Jews continue to stand in a special relationship with God. Christianity introduces the anti-thesis that proclaims that Jesus, through his willingness to sacrifice himself, has altered the old covenant. The new covenant is affirmed by "new blood" by the blood of God's son. Instead of Abraham it is Jesus through whom God has established a new covenant.* (In Hebrew the New Testament is called Brith Hachadashah, that is, the New Covenant.) In fact, Paul proposes that circumcision of the penis is no longer necessary, for it is through Jesus that one achieves true circumcision, that is, the circumcision of the heart. (Corinthians

Faith and Conflict

7:19) It is through faith in Jesus, not through circumcision, that one becomes a part of the new covenant where salvation is given to all who accept Jesus as the Son of God. Thus by negating the legitimacy of the old covenant, Christianity also negates the legitimacy of Judaism as a religion.

But unlike Jesus' death and declaration of faith that is the only condition to the Christian covenant Jews have an additional element to their covenant one that began with Abraham and was reinforced at Sinai.

Abraham: the foundation universal morality

Abraham's argument with God regarding the destruction of Sodom and Gomorrah is a declaration that faith alone is not adequate to achieve salvation. God demands not only faith but above all else He demands moral behavior. In fact God's demand for morality precedes the requirement of faith is evident that Abraham's discourse with God regarding the cities of Sodom and Gomorrah precedes that of Isaac's sacrifice. The story of Sodom and Gomorrah starts with God musing to himself as he raises the following hypothetical question, "Shall I hide anything that I may do from Abraham? " (Genesis18:17) God proceeds to tell Abraham his plan to destroy the two cities because of the cry of those upon whom the Sodomites have inflicted injustice. Through the destruction of the two cities, God seeks to reiterate the significance of moral behavior to Abraham so that he will teach his household righteousness and justice. (Genesis:18:19). Abraham, out of love of humanity and full of mercy, seeks to soften God's judgment. He gets God's promise that if there are even as few as ten righteous people He will not destroy the two cities. God will not destroy the righteous with the guilty. Here we encounter Abraham's universalism when he confronts God by asking: Will not God judge all the earth justly? (Genesis:18:25) [Emphasis added]

Through this story we encounter the Jewish view (1) that morality founded on the principle of justice is more important to God than faith, (2) that God himself must adhere to the same principles of justice that He imposes upon people and, (3) that all people will stand before God and be judged not so much for their faith but for their adherence to the law of justice.

With its emphasis on justice, Judaism introduces the principle of accountability. Jews relationship with God is based on a covenant, a contract, in which both sides assume obligations to each other. There are numerous stories in which God is called to account for his actions. In the story of Sodom and Gomorrah, God justifies his actions pointing out that the people in these cities have violated the most fundamental commandment that is, humanity's obligation to adhere to the principles of justice and justice demands that people should be held accountable for their behavior. As a response to this demand Judaism has set aside the days of awe during which, according to Jewish belief, all people stand in judgment before God the Judge and are held accountable for their violation of moral laws and not for their faith.

Jewish view of accountability is founded on their belief in the supremacy of the moral law. The principle of accountability requires that we have clear standards specific moral laws that serve as standards by which a person's behavior can be judged. Judgment and accountability, however, are absent in the Christian view of man -god relationship. Christianity does not have a clear set of laws other than the very vague "law of love" to which they should adhere. But even in this regard, the law of love is suggestive and not compulsory. Hence Christians are not held accountable whether they violate the suggested principle of love.

Faith and Conflict

Christian-Jewish Dialectic

To understand the complex dialectic relationship between the Jewish and Christian belief systems, we must point out that when Paul formalized Christian theology, he rejected the Torah. He also rejected the Jewish belief of the continued existence of the covenant through circumcision that God forged with Abraham. In so doing Paul not only created a schism between Judaism and Christianity, but he also excused Christians from obeying the laws specified in the Torah including the moral law therein. Paul excused Christians from the obligatory nature of the standards to which Jews are expected to adhere in their interpersonal relationships.

Paul's rejection of the legitimacy of the covenant between God and Abraham is founded in his desire to make Christianity independent from Judaism. Paul sought to eliminate the significance of God's promise to Abraham and to his descendants which he made after testing Abraham's faith. The terms of the covenant are that God will bless and multiply Abraham's seed and make them as multitudinous as the stars in heaven ....and through Abraham's seed shall all the nations will be blessed. (Genesis 22:18) This view stands in opposition to the one advocated by Christianity, namely, that is through Christ that people will be blessed. Although Abraham is rewarded for his faith, at the same time God however places greater credence on morality than faith for achieving salvation. This is expressed in the story where Abraham confronts God regarding Sodom and Gomorrah. This story informs us that, in the final analysis, God's goodness is not bestowed on the faithful without their adhering to morality. In the Jewish view salvation is the reward one receives for his moral behavior and not for faith alone. When Abraham bargains with God regarding the fate of Sodom and Gomorrah, the issue of faith does not enter into the discourse. Faith seems to be immaterial when God judges humanity. Both individuals and societies are judged solely on their adherence to moral principles that is founded on justice. This principle is exampled in the following rabbinic tale.

Rabbinic legends tell that Sodom was governed by four judges: Sharkai-the liar, Shakurai – the arch deceiver, Zayyefai – the forger, and Matzle-dina – perverter of justice. In another story the Talmudic rabbis sought to illustrate that the two cities sins that led to their demise was their practice of injustice and not faith. The story revolves around two maidens that went down to draw water from a well. One asked the other.: "Why is your face so sickly?" The other answered: "We have no food left, and we are about to die." What did the first one do? She filled her own pitcher with flour, and the two exchanged pitchers, each taking the others. So great was the Sodomites rejection of justice that when they became aware of this, they seized the maiden who saved the others life and burned her alive. The Holy one said, "Even if I wished to remain silent, justice for the maiden does not allow me to do so." (Bialik and Ravnizky p. 27). This story, reiterates God's response to Cain: The voice of your brother's blood cries unto me from the ground." The violation and perversion of justice cannot be atoned by shedding the blood of an animal, of a human, or of another God.

Similarly, in the story of Jonah, we are also told that God intended to destroy the city of Nineveh not because of their faithlessness but because of their wickedness. Nineveh was, as the prophet Nahum called it, a bloody city, the capital of a nation that placed primacy on the subjugation of others and not on justice.

The primacy of moral behavior is elaborated in the book of Exodus. Morality consists of norms that guide man-man and man-nature relationships. The common feature of the moral ordinances is that they are founded on the principle of justice. In ancient Judaism the guardians of moral behavior were the prophets. Nathan is the model of the moral prophet a person who abhors the abuse of power. It is he who challenges David's behavior because of his arbitrary use of power in

Faith and Conflict

acquiring Bathsheba. David was faithful to God; he dutifully offered his sacrifices, but because he acted unjustly Nathan stood up against him.

The significance of moral behavior and its pre-eminence over faith and rituals such as sacrifices are reiterated by Isaiah. In the first chapter Isaiah sets the tone for his prophetic mission. He addresses Judah and its people and leadership whom he calls "the rulers of Sodom." and the people as the "people of Gomorrah" (1:10). He derides them not for the absence of faith but for their evil ways that which is the absence of justice. Speaking for YHVEH he queries: To what purpose is the multitudes of our sacrifices. Instead of fat bullocks, he proposes what God wants us to seek justice and to relieve the oppressed. This, Isaiah proposes, is not only required from Judeans but from all nations. It is deeds of justice that bring salvation both to nations and to its people. It is only moral behavior Isaiah declares in Chapter 56 will result in salvation to all including eunuchs and aliens who may believe in or serve other gods.

Immoral behavior, Isaiah proclaims in the name of God, cannot be atoned for by the offering of fat bullocks, turtle doves or, for that matter, any forms of offering. God cannot be bribed nor bought. He does not need, or require, our prophets declare, cultic religious expression of sacrifice and perhaps not even a declaration of faith.

Faith is most often particularistic and it differs between people's experiences with God and with nature. Moral behavior, on the other hand is universal. While faith is a passive relationship with God and requires the expression of belief and unquestioned trust in God, moral behavior, on the other hand requires proper action between people. It requires that one's interpersonal relationships should be based on justice. Faith does not require accountability whereas morals do. More importantly, faith demands the love God whereas morals require the love of justice.

Moral Authority

Durkheim, one of the fathers of modern sociology, finds that no collectivity can exist without adherence to a moral authority. Moral rules, Durkheim proposes, "have an imperative character to the extent that exercise a sort of ascendancy over the will which constrains [the individual] to conform to them." (Cours de science sociale p.42) Morals have an internal psychological power that compels the adherence to behave justly. Moreover, both the power of morality and its legitimacy are derived from some ascendant entity real or ideal but one that is superior to us individuals. In Judaism, this ascendant power lies in God who demands accountability. As a child, for instance, I was taught that every night while sleeping my soul ascends to heaven and there I wrote down, in a book like a ledger, all my deeds for that day. In time I will be held accountable for these deeds. In fact, Jews have set aside the ten days between Rosh Hashanah and Yom Kippur when each person, Jew and non-Jew alike, is being judged to the extent to which they adhered to the moral mitzvoth – the moral commandments. The quality of life one enjoys in this world and salvation in the next must be earned by one's deeds in this world. Salvation in the next world, Jewish theology expounds, is not a gift but the reward for behavior. Rabbi Yehuda Hanasi, one of the Talmudic sages, tells us: Consider the following three things and you will avoid coming into the grip of sin – know what is above you: a seeing eye, a hearing ear and all your deeds are recorded in the book. (Talmud "Ethics of our Father" 2:1).

Judaism's demand for moral behavior and accountability for the achievement of salvation would have been detrimental to Paul's attempt to Christianize the non-Jewish world. Obeying the Law with all its demands on moral obedience is difficult. However, when Paul rejects the need to comply with the Torah, he also rejects the special relationship that Jews forged with God at Mount Sinai. Instead, Paul

Faith and Conflict

offers a new covenant one based solely on faith in Christ. The new covenant retains the old idea of being a chosen people but being chosen now is given only of those who accept Christ. Through faith in Christ the adherents will become the new chosen people, a people beloved by God.

This, of course, is unlike Judaism that demands obedience to the Torah as sine qua non of becoming a member of the Jewish community. Christians demand only a declaration of faith to Christ. Unlike Judaism where giving "Tzedakah" (loosely translated as charity) is a moral obligation Christianity makes charity a personal choice. Charity in Christianity is given as an exercise in free will. It is only because of their love of Christ should one minister to the needy. Charity to the poor is based on Christ's teaching that as they did to him so they should do the least of others. Christianity does not obligate their adherents to give charity. It is unlike the laws that obligate land owners to leave the corners of the fields for the poor. Any sin either committed by commission or omission is rectified by one thing and that is by accepting Jesus. For those who have faith in Jesus and are baptized through him will become sinless, saved through grace of God and will have life everlasting.

In his letter to the Ephesians (2:8,9) Paul tells that "For by grace are ye saved through faith; and that not of yourselves: it is the gift of God: Not of works, lest any man should boast for we are his workmanship, created in Christ Jesus unto good works, which God has ordained that we should walk in them." (Ephesians 2:8-10) In his epistle to Titus Paul writes: Not by works of righteousness which we have done, but according to his mercy he saved us, by the washing of regeneration, and renewing of the Holy Ghost; which he shed on us abundantly through Jesus Christ our savior. (Titus3:5-6)

While Judaism stresses morals based on justice as the guide for interpersonal relationship, Christianity has instead chosen to stress interpersonal love. In Christianity love of God and of people has become the foundation on which human relationships are to be based. It is not my intention to denigrate the significance of love but unlike morals it lacks both specificity and moral authority. (I have already discussed the weakness of love as a guide line for interpersonal relationships. See the essay on Love and Justice in this book.) Love is at best a suggestive ideal, a social and religious value, but it does not have the imperative character that the specific morals enumerated in the book of Exodus have.

The command to love one's neighbor is not foreign to Jews. After all, it was first stated in Leviticus (19:18). Moreover, the text also proposes that to be able to love one first must empty his heart from hatred. (Leviticus 19:17) The law of loving one's neighbor was taught by Rabbi Hillel (30 b.c.e-3 C.E. who lived somewhat earlier than Christ), who declared that love is the essence of Judaism. But love alone is inadequate for it does not demand the exercise of justice. The commandments in Exodus and Deuteronomy do not that state that people should treat each other justly just because they love the other. There are human relationships, for instance contractual relationships, which are based on justice alone. These laws specify how one must treat the poor, the workers, the powerless and even animals. It is not necessary, although it may be desirable, that we should love the blind, the deaf, the widowed, the orphaned, and the workers, but is paramount is that we should regardless of love not violate their rights. Rights are not something that one gives to another because of love. Rights and justice are entitlements and they are independent of love.

Unlike the Jewish imperative of justice, Christianity places emphasis solely on love which lacks the inalienability and the universality contained in laws. Many Christians point to the injunction "love your enemy" as evidence of universal love. But, does it? Does "love your enemy" really imply that love must be offered and be given to all humanity even to one's enemies? Feuerbach doesn't think so. Feuerbach's interpretation of the dictum to love one's enemy is one that he derived from Luther and the Christian Bible. He proposes that the teaching to love one's enemies has reference only to personal enemies and not to the enemies of God, the enemies of Christ, to the unbelievers. For instance one cannot love the enemy of Christ for "he who loves the men whom Christ denies, does [himself] not believe Christ, [and] denies his Lord and God." An emphasis on faith in Christ, Feuerbach proposes, abolishes any natural ties that one may have to each other as human beings; it abolishes our view of universal unity, the natural unity of mankind, and instead it substitutes a particular unity." (Feuerbach p.254) In short Christian faith, because it rejects the right of unbelievers to salvation, denies the unity of mankind and of human universalism. "Faith" Feuerbach proposes "knows only friends or enemies, it understand no neutrality; it is preoccupied only with itself." (Feurbach 1957 p.255)

Accountability and Reparation:

The corollary to accountability is rectification. In Judaism rectification is bifurcated. We believe in a dual world: the world of heaven which is the domain of God and the human world which belongs to mankind. In Psalm 115, the psalmist declares: The heavens are the heavens of the Lord; but the earth He has given to the children of men. Hence in Judaism the bifurcation is not between God and Caesar but between God and humankind. Thus sins are also bifurcated, there are sins that one commits against God and sins one commits against mankind. Therefore, rectification of wrongs must also be directed in two directions. We seek forgiveness from God for the wrongs that we commit against Him when we violate His ordained rituals and commandments.

However, we must rectify and repair the wrongs committed against each other by seeking forgiveness from the people whom we wronged on whom we inflicted pain.

Confession and rectification in Christianity is, contrarily, a unidirectional relationship between the sinner and God. While in Judaism, God cannot forgive one who committed a wrong against his fellow man. In Christianity, for instance, during confession the priest may grant absolution for all manner of sins. Theoretically priests function in the name of or as a substitute for God. There is no demand for true rectification for sins committed against fellow man. All sins in the final analysis are sins committed against God, hence God through his priests can grant atonement and absolution for all sins. This was the foundation on which the priests claimed legitimacy for and the validity of the indulgences they sold. Even when "temporal punishment" was required, this could be achieved through good works and not necessarily by re-establishing status ante quo. In short the sinner is not required to confront the person whom he wronged and make restitution to him—that is to make the victim whole.

As a graduate teaching assistant I taught sociology courses in prisons where I became aware of the prisoners common mantra: If you accept Christ all your sins are forgiven and you will merit salvation. No mention has ever been made about the need for receiving forgiveness from the victim or his family, and the corollary, the need to rectify the wrong that has been committed.

Christian stress on redemption by faith has led Christians to deviate from the traditional Jewish conception of penance. In Judaism penance is the act of returning (t'shuvah) to God's moral ordinances to the mitzvot. Penance is achieved through deeds. The remission of sins is achieved only through changing one's behavior. If the sins one commits are against other persons, their remission can only occur if the sinner brings back status ante quo; that is, if one re-establishes the a priori conditions that has been altered by the sinner's action.

Faith and Conflict

This idea is very similar to Durkheim's description of the social-moral conditions in a society under an organic solidarity. (See: Durkheim The Division of Labor in Society) It seems to me that this is not central in Christianity. Paul advises the Apostles thusly: Repent, and be baptized every one of you in the name of Jesus Christ for the remission of sins, and ye shall receive the gift of the Holy Ghost." (Acts 2:38) This gift is not only salvation but also being freed from sin. For there is only one way to God's salvation and being cleansed from sin and that is through faith in Jesus Christ as the Savior. If anyone tells you otherwise, they are liars they are the spirit of the anti-Christ. (1John 4:2-3) This quote from John demonstrates that there is no need for accountability of wrongs committed against other humans and even more importantly, one doesn't have to make reparations to the wronged. Forgiveness is a part of the assumption of faith – it is a gift – regardless what sins are for which the sinner seeks absolution. Jewish belief, in contrast, holds that when God proclaimed that He remembers the sins of fathers unto the third and fourth generations, it merely indicates that no sin can be forgiven by God until the wrongs against the other has been repaired and been rectified.

Summary and conclusion:

Summary and conclusion:

The question that is paramount to me is: Has the absence of accountability in Christianity contributed to historic Christian hostility against Jews and ultimately to the existence of the Holocaust? An emphasis on faith, as it exists in Christianity (and perhaps in Islam), leads to the insistence that the believers must become the defenders of God. (In the Middle Ages monarchs were also seen as the defenders of the faith.) In defending one's faith one also becomes hostile to those who question the legitimacy of the defender's faith. That is the only act for which the faithful can be held accountable. No Christian is held accountable for harming another in his attempt to defend his faith. No Christian can be held accountable for his hostility to and for the harm that one commits as a defender of his faith against non-believers. This view is similar to Goldwater's view that excesses in the defense of liberty can be a virtue.

I wonder whether the harsh life and the loss of millions of Jewish lives that Jews experienced in the last two millennia would have existed if Christianity would have continued the Jewish tradition: the demand for accountability for their treatment to their fellow men especially those of other faiths? Let me hasten to state Christianity also demands accountability but as a faith based god-centered religion Christianity demands accountability for their faith in Jesus. Judaism while it also emphasizes belief it bases primacy on homocentric morals and makes adherence to moral principles, and not faiths, the sine qua non for salvation. In the theo-centric religions people are held accountable for their unquestioned faith in and adherence to God or Gods while in homocentric religions accountability is based on adherence to the principles of moral justice. I wonder would the Holocaust have existed if Paul would not have substituted the primacy of faith for moral accountability. Feuerbach is right when he observed that Christian doctrine stresses that we owe more to God than we do to humanity. Unfortunately, the more we become concerned with God's needs, we become less concerned with human needs

Let me suggest that what people of the world, regardless of their faith, religion should teach that we owe each other is not love but justice. Faith is a wonderful state of existence and brings peace to the individual but it is only justice that can bring peace to the world. The prince of peace must also be the prince of justice and not necessarily the prince of love.

Notes

* Substituting animals for human life is continued even today among the Orthodox Jews. Before Yom Kippur one uses chickens to offer their lives instead of humans. Holding the chicken (i.e. a hen for a female and a rooster for a male) one recites the following: This is my exchange, this is my atonement, this chicken will go to his death and I will have good life and a peaceful one.

References

1. Bialik Hayim N. and Ravnitzky Y.H. 1992 The Book of Legends (trans. W.G. Braude) N.Y. Schoken Books
2. Carroll, James, 2001 Constantine's Sword: The Church and the Jews, Boston Houghton Mifflin Co.
3. Durkheim Emile.1982 The Rules of Sociological Method (trans. W.D.Halls) New York, The Free Press.

Summary and conclusion:

4. Durkheim, Emile 1984 The Division of Labor in Society (trans. W.D.Halls) The Free Press
5. Feuerbach, Ludwig (1957) The Essence of Christianity N.Y. Harper Torch Books.
6. The Mishnah : The Ethics of our Fathers. Willis, Gary, 2000, The Papal Sin: Structures of Deceit. New York Double Day.
7. Passelecq, G. and Suchecky, B. The Hidden Encyclical of Pius XI, 1997,Orlando, Harcourt Brace and Company. 92

Love and Justice*
Foundation of Jewish and
Christian Values

In 1972 I attended the annual meeting of the Georgia Sociological Association in Savannah. In one of the sessions a professor who was also a minister of the Gospel gave a paper in which he kept on referring to Judeo-Christian ethics and morals. At the end of his presentation during the question and answer period I strongly disagreed with the speaker. "Professor" I told him "in spite of the common usage of the term Judeo-Christian Morals and values it is a fallacious concept. Jews and Christians differ in their world views. In fact Christian values and ideals stand in a dialectical relationship with Jewish values. Christian values have arisen out of a different economic and political infrastructure than did the much earlier values in Judaism. These differences may suggest that Christian values stand in a dialectical relationship with the Jewish ones they became an opponent and the negation of the Jewish values.

Jewish and Christian values began to differ when Paul summarily dismissed the law and circumcision that were and still are the most significant elements to Jewish identity. Even more important is the fact that for the last two thousand years Jews in the Christian world have occupied a subordinate social and economic position and were frequently

Faith and Conflict

ejected from many Christian countries and in others they were forced to live in Ghettos and in constant fear for their lives. However, even most importantly, the Christian experiences in the Roman Empire led them to reject the foundation of the Jewish value system that resides in the Torah and paved for themselves not only a different faith but also values."

Of course my comments created a great disturbance. With these words I rejected the idea of the commonality of the three faiths a unity that presumptuously is founded on the idea that members of the three faiths: Judaism, Christianity, and Islam are the descendants of Abraham and his faith. My proposition that Judaism and Christianity have different core values challenged the foundation on which Christianity has for two millennia based its legitimacy. When Christians speak of the Bible they proclaim the unity of both the Christian and Jewish Bible. In this sense Christians seek to usurp Jewish beliefs and stress that not only are all the Jewish values contained in the Christian belief but with having a new covenant with God they ascend Judaism. The following episode will clearly demonstrate this point.

In my sophomore year at Washington University I participated in a class discussion of the relationship between religion and values. When the class was over a student in my class continued the discussion with me as I walked to my next class. In our conversation, to support my claim I quoted a biblical passage. "What Bible are you quoting from?" he inquired. I was startled. Indeed what Bible am I quoting? I sought that there was but one Bible. So I responded to his query. "I am quoting from the Old Testament. In fact" I informed him "since I am very familiar with the Bible in its original Hebrew my quote is a direct translation of the Hebrew text." "Since you are not quoting the Catholic Bible I cannot accept your statement as valid." This statement severed our discussion because he could not accept the idea of the singularity of the Bible.

If we are to understand each other, and if we seek a way to be able to live with each other in harmony we must understand each other's values. Values create a frame of reference by which we interpret reality. Because of this when we are seeking solutions to social problems values will gives a particular focus and direct our attention to on a set of possible solutions and distract our perception from possible other solutions. To understand Jewish – Christian differences we need to understand not only the common elements and similarities in these two faiths but perhaps even more importantly their differences.

Jewish–Christian differences are rooted in the emphasis they place on Biblical teachings. Judaism places primacy on the teaching of the Old Testament (from now on to be referred to as the Jewish Bible) with its emphasis on justice and the contractual relationship with God also known as "the covenant." Christianity, on the other hand, places primacy on the teachings found in the New Testament (the Christian Bible) with an emphasis on the idea of love. Let me hasten to point out that I do not imply that love as a value ideal is absent in Judaism or that Christianity rejects the ideal of justice. After all, the importance of love started with the declaration in Exodus "Thou shall love thy neighbor as thyself." Hillel (30B.C.E– 9C.E paraphrased and elaborated the above statement and gave us the following teaching: "What is hateful to thee, do not do unto thy fellow man; this is the law; the rest is commentary; study it." This teaching has become the foundation of the Christian concept of love as declared in the Christian Bible.

However, if we closely examine the Jewish teaching one finds that justice supersedes love in Judaism and that love supersedes all other values in Christianity. (In fact the word justice does not appear in the concordance of the Christian Bible. More about this will be discussed later.) The Christian Bible promotes love as the essence of Christianity: "For God so loved the world, that he gave his only begotten Son… "(John 3:16) Furthermore John sees God and love as interchangeable ideals: "He that loveth not knoweth not God; for God is love (John 4:8). Love in the Christian theology transcends all norms; it is the ultimate

Faith and Conflict

of all commandments: "Owe no man anything, but love one another: for he that loveth another hath fulfilled the law. (Romans 13:8)

In examination of love as an ideal I placed primacy on the effects love on intra and inter group relationship. In this paper I am not seeking to define love instead I am focusing on behavior that is prescribed by the Christian view of love. Matthew (26:35) quotes Jesus who reflects on what his disciples did to him because they loved him. Jesus says: For I was hungered, and ye gave me meat: I was thirsty and ye gave me drink; I was a stranger and ye took me in; and ye clothed me; I was sick, and ye visited me; I was in prison, and ye came to me. This passage suggests that love, at least from Jesus' perspective, is manifested through ministration; if one loves another, one shows it by his concern for the other's welfare, by his desire to alleviate the other's pain, whether it is that of the body or the soul. Through love one is able to commiserate, empathize, and respond to the needs of others. Thus when help is to be bestowed it takes the form of charity. The help one gives another is the consequence of empathy. Charitable action that is directed to others in need that arises out of love, empathy and the concern for others places emphasis on treating and alleviating the suffering of the individual in trouble rather than seeking the source of the problem and preventing it from happening. The most common activities of Christian missionaries, for instance, are feeding the hungry and treating the sick rather than altering the system that brings hunger or the conditions that brings sickness. Such charitable acts are post facto solutions of problems and as such it merely perpetuates the conditions that made charity necessary.

However, help that is given as charity in response to the command to love lacks dependability; it is capricious because any help given for the sake of love is given as a "freewill offering." The desire to help others comes because the giver "feels for" and emphasizes with other human beings in need. This emotional foundation of charity is often seen as acts of Christian love. They cannot be commanded as are morals. To "love one another" is merely a value and not a moral norm for love that is having this feeling for another cannot be legislated or commanded. Love is not bestowed to everyone alike. Feuerbach points out that the Christian injunction to love is particularistic value. He proposes that "To love the man who does not believe in Christ is a sin against Christ, is to love the enemy of Christ. That which God, which Christ does not love, man must not love; his love would be a contradiction of the divine will, consequently a sin." Faith, which by its very nature is particularistic, restricts or limits the bestowing love to those outside of faithful. Feuerbach explains: (254)The Maxim "Love your enemies" has reference to personal enemies, not to public enemies, the enemies of God, the enemies of faith, to the unbelievers. He who loves the men whom Christ denies, does not believe in Christ, (he) denies his Lord and God. **Faith abolishes the natural ties of humanity; natural unity, it substitutes a particular unity.** (Emphasis added)

(We clearly see that love is not bestowed equally but differentially depending upon the donor's decision as to who merits it and thus the help that is allocated is particularistic. In other words, love leads us to judge each individual and his problem. Christian charity hence often differentiates between those who merit our help from those who do not. How often have we heard that we should not be concerned with those who are suffering from AIDS, they do not merit our help because their suffering is the consequence of the sins they committed. Their illness is God's punishment for their moral violation.

Charity that is based on love is concerned with helping the individual overcome his problem. Such a charity distracts out attention the social system as a whole and most importantly from the prevention of the problem especially if the problem lies in the system and its solution requires the changing of the system. Charity, in the Christian sense, is concerned not with the solution of the problem but with ameliorating a post facto condition. Durkheim's remark about charity is most apropos. He writes (1962:58) Charity "organized nothing. It maintains the

Faith and Conflict

status quo; it can attenuate the individual suffering that this [economic system's] lack of organization engenders."

In contrast to Christianity, Judaism stresses two moral values justice and love but, justice is the pinnacle of all values. Its importance in the Jewish cultural system is evident from the fact that justice is perceived as the foundation of life: Justice, justice shalt thou pursue that you mayest live. (Deut.16:20) Of the three paramount values demanded by the deity, justice is first; it stands above mercy and humility (Micah 6:8). Justice, explains Rabbi Hertz (1937:928), is independent of the seat of power; it stands above the monarchy so that the regulations concerning justice precede those concerning the appointments of kings. Justice and law are two distinct phenomena; the former is independent of power but those in power and those who rule are subject to its pre and proscriptions. So important is this value that in the name of justice one can question even God's actions.** Of course Judaism also subscribes to the principle of love to the extent that Rabbi Hillel declared the essence of the Torah lies in the statement "Thou shall love thy neighbor as thyself" the rest is commentary. Still, it is my view that justice precedes love as the principal moral value.

What is the Jewish Bible's definition of justice? What does it connote? Here, too, we will seek an answer not by a definition but by the prescriptions that reflect this principle. Above all, justice seeks to prescribe equity in asymmetrical power relationships, e.g., "And you shall judge with justice between man and his brother and the stranger" (Deut.1:17) It specifies further that an equitable relationship should exist between the poor and the mighty.*** Justice, then, consists of moral values that seek to guard power abuse especially in economic situations and in the courts. Moreover, justice also determines not only man-man relationships but also the ones between man and beast. For instance, the principles of justice define the laws of money lending especially the control the lender can exercise over various collaterals. The hirer of labor is told that he may not withhold the laborers wages over night. With regards to animals we are instructed that one cannot harness two different animals together especially when the weaker animal will be required to work as hard as the stronger.

As a human value the Biblical and hence the Jewish principle of justice stresses the idea that human relationships should be governed by a set of universally defined duties and privileges that cannot be altered or abused by an asymmetrical power relationship. We find, for instance, that Nathan the prophet chastises and condemns the powerful monarch David because he abused his power and thereby committed injustice. Similarly Jeremiah admonishes the rulers, and Isaiah rebukes the priests because of power abuse.

The Prophets have thus legitimated their right to question and criticize the powerful persons: the kings, the wealthy, and the priests. The tradition established by the prophets has also led to the legitimacy of questioning the society as a whole that fosters and permits the abuse of power. In other words, when justice became the dominant and fundamental value the critical examination and challenge of the social system is encouraged. The social critics having thus gained status became the vigilant guards for maintaining a just system and guards against those who sought to abuse their power. In fact one can easily see how Jesus followed in the prophets foot-steps and sought to become and to re-establish the just social system that has been eroding in the post Herodian society.****

Unlike love that encourages a particularistic relationship between members of a social system, justice demands a universalistic orientation and prescribes that all relationships, outside of familial relationships, should be guided by the moral of equitable reciprocity. In sum, while love directs attention toward the individual and toward alleviating the individual's problem through personal charity, justice directs our attention to power relationships. It directs our attention toward power inequities in the system and to the problems that result from such inequities, and seeks the solution not necessarily with helping the

Faith and Conflict

individual but with the solution of the problem within the system that caused the social problems in the first place. Among the concerns that rise from and are associated with the principle of social justice is related to people's right to a chance to life, that is to have access to means of production.

Thus we see that Jewish value system consist both with the prescription to love another and to do justice. This dual value system hence has created in the ancient Jewish society two different forms of charity. The charity that arises out of a concern for loving your neighbor is called in Hebrew "gemilath chassadim" i.e. the practice of kind acts. This is essentially very similar to Jesus' statement what has been done to him. The practice of kindness includes feeding the hungry, hospitality to strangers, visiting the sick, dowering the bride, attending the dead to the grave, the making of peace between fellow men, and the freeing of the slaves (i.e. the imprisoned). These are values that are associated with human kindness. There is no limit prescribed to their performance. Those who perform such acts will reap rewards in the world to come, that is salvation in their life after death but those who do not perform acts of kindness will be neither rewarded nor will they be punished. Gemilath chasadim are free will acts they are not commanded they are suggested.

In contrast to acts of kindness Judaism also prescribes charity as a moral norm. Such acts of charity are proscriptive; they are commandments that have to be performed. They are duties to the givers and privileges for the receivers. The Hebrew word for this type of charity is Tzedokoh which is a derivative of Tzadok from which the following words are also derived: Tzedek (justice) and Tzadik (righteousness, or a righteous person). In other words, charity (Tzedokoh) is justice in action, that is activities that are related for the maintenance of justice, namely, an equity relationship between the poor and the mighty in which it is the duty of the mighty to be taxed so that the poor can be given a chance to life. The concept "Tzedokoh" represents the idea of "just due" and it implies that poor people have the right to expect help. Such help is not given merely as an empathetic response as one's personal concern for another's plight. It is not a free will offering; tzedokoh is an obligation that must be given to the poor and it assures that the poor will have a chance to life. For example, in ancient Israel it was the poor person's right to harvest the corners of the field and to pick up the stalks of wheat after the gleaners. The owner of the field, by law, had to leave the corners of field un-harvested and could not determine which of the poor persons could come to harvest the corners of his field. In more recent times a certain portion of the money that is paid in the purchase of "matzoth" the unleavened bread used for Passover (maoth chitin) is used to provide the necessary foods to the poor so that they too could perform the Passover ceremony. Such forms of charity are normative; they are not acts of free will. Those who violated these acts in the past were sanctioned. Tzedokoh, thus, is a part of the Jewish legal system.

Jewish charity, both as a free will offering and most importantly the norm of charity has left its imprint on the present Jewish culture. The consequence of these values and norms is that Jews have maintained a liberal political perspective. It is interesting to note that unlike many Christians when they become wealthy and upwardly mobile have often changed political membership from being Democratic to the Republican Party. Jews, on the other hand, tend to maintain their Democratic political affiliation a perspective that may come closest to the spirit of "Tzedokoh."

It was my intention in this paper to show the roots of liberal Weltanschauungen that dominates the Jewish socio-political views and in a way stand in a dialectical relationship with the Christian value of love. I have argued, and I hope cogently, that Jews and Christians differ in their dominant values and hence it would be erroneous to imply the existence of a Judeo-Christian normative and ethical system. While Judaism and Christianity may share the idea of love as value guide for

Faith and Conflict

inter-personal relationships Jews however place greater emphasis on the norm of justice – a value that is absent in the Christian Bible. (For an in depth discussion of this subject see the next article in this book.) But even the idea of love differs between the Christian and Jewish concept. I have shown that Christian view of love is highly particularistic and it is to be bestowed only on those who share a commitment to the principles of Christianity. Those who are not baptized as declared in the Christian Bible are damned by God. Of course if God does not love them why then should mortals – that is, Christians love them? In contrast Judaism does not deny salvation on the basis of belief. Salvation is given on the basis of adherence to moral order be one a Jew or non-Jew. Hence, we not only love but we also honor those individuals who are defined by Jews as righteous gentiles – those who saved Jewish lives during the Holocaust. He who saves one life, the Talmud declares, is as though he saved the whole world. This holds true for Jew and non-Jew alike.

I have also argued that love directs attention to the individual and his problem and not to the possibility that these problems have their origin in the social system itself.***** More recently there has been an attempt by some Christian ministers to return to the teaching of the Jewish Bible and start emphasizing and re-interpreting justice as "love in action." (Wallis, 2005 and Marsh, 2005)

The realization that love as means of altering the social system is inadequate Christian ministers have lately increased reliance on Prophetic language in the Jewish Bible with their emphasis on justice. For instance this was central in the pastoral letter issued by 16 Bishops of the Third World titled: Gospel and Revolution (Lewy, 1974 p.i). They proclaim:

It is not true that God wishes there to be rich men enjoying the good Things of this world by exploiting the poor: it is not true that God wishes there to be poor people always wretched. ... Christians and their pastors should know to recognize the hand of the Almighty in those events that from time to time put down the mighty from their thrones and raise the humble, send away the rich empty handed, and fill the hungry with good things.

The language here is similar to that of Micah or of Isaiah the language of those who place justice above the traditional view of love. Moreover, the content of the letter rejects poverty as a desirable state that assures the poor and the humble eventual power if only they would wait for the Day of Judgment to come.

This idea that was central to the liberation theology has been rejected by the recent Pope.. In his Papal Encyclical "Deus Caritas Est" The Holy See reaffirms that supremacy of individual and personal love. In short the essential differences in Christian Jewish values remain the same as before.

Notes:

*This is a revised version of a paper published earlier in the Review of Religious Research 16:No.1 pp 41-46 (Fall 1974)

**There are a number of Talmudic and Chassidic tales in which victims sought to bring God to a Beth Din (Courthouse) because in their view God has not acted justly. This starts when Abraham argued with God whether God is justified in his desire to destroy the cities of Sodom and Gomorrah.

*** The word mighty refers to the wealthy who control the means of production.

**** Power is used here in two senses: first, as the capacity of an individual to influence and affect the behavior of others; and second as the extent to which one controls scarce resources.

Faith and Conflict

***** The focus on the individual is also mirrored in the Christian concern for personal salvation and for individual morality such as sex, drinking, and gambling. It is only recently that some Christian activists have focused their attention on the economic and political order. When they do they use the Jewish Bible and particularly the Prophets as their moral mentors. (See Hill, 1964)

References:

1. Durkheim, Emile, 1962, Socialism. Translated by Charlotte Sattler. New York. N.Y. Collier Books
2. Feuerbach, Ludwig, 1957, The Essence of Christianity. Translated by George Eliot. New York N.Y. Harper Torch Books, Harper and Row Publishers.
3. Hertz, J.H.(ed), 1937, The Pentateuch. London, Eng. Lowe and Bryndon Ltd.
4. Hill, Samuel S., 1964, "Southern Protestantism and racial integration." Religion in Life 33:421-429
5. Lewy, Guenter, 1974, Religion and Revolution. New York, Oxford University Press.
6. Marsh, Carles, 2005, Beloved Community. New York, N.Y. Basic Books
7. Wallis, Jim, 2005, God's Politics, New York, N.Y. HarperCollins Pub. 104

Justice: The illusive concept in Christian Theology (1)

Christianity and Geo-political Conditions

In the previous essay I examined the differences in the Jewish and Christian fundamental values. I proposed that while Jewish values are founded on the Biblical principle of justice Christianity, on the other hand, chose the Christian Bible's emphasis on love to become the infrastructure of their values. I pointed out that a commitment to justice is associated with political perspective than a commitment to love. I proposed that a commitment to justice will, in today's perspective, more likely to be associated with political liberalism while love is often used to justify and support the political status quo – hence political conservatism. Lewy examining the relationship between religion and revolution proposes that ideologies that support political power seek to legitimate their perspective by stressing the "transcendent moral standards which define an ideal against which human performance can be measured. (Lewy 1974:458-6) The religious perspective of love seeks to help the individuals who are experiencing difficulties. Those who are committed to and place primacy on love, as Jesus commanded, emphasize the feeding of the hungry and clothing the naked but they hardly ever challenge the system that produces hunger or fails

Faith and Conflict

to provide clothing or shelter. It is this view that has kept religion, especially Christianity, from becoming a revolutionary force. I admit that there were some occasions when Christians following the teachings of the Old Testament prophets have become a revolutionary force. Such a revolutionary force, for instance, was the Peasant Revolution of 1532. Munzer a theologian and leader of this revolution often referred to the Prophetic teachings and ideals and saw himself as the reincarnation of Daniel. Similarly in the last century the advocates of the Liberation Theology have also presented themselves in the mold of Old Testament prophets and speaking in their idiomatic language they too, like the Jewish prophets, placed justice ahead of love. No wonder thence that Liberation Theology was not supported by the Vatican.

In 1967 I was commissioned by ministerial association of White Heaven, a suburb of Memphis (TN) to ascertain what the population of that community considered to be the issues that should be central to the Christian ministers concern. This study was conducted during the height of the War in Vietnam. The survey data that I gathered shows that the respondent felt that ministers should occupy themselves with social and not with political issues. Ministers, the respondents indicated should follow the teaching of Christian love which in their view was to be concerned with personal problems such as divorce, alcoholism, gambling, and with helping the poor. Ministers should not be concerned in their sermons with the war or with matters of election.

By contrast among the above mentioned respondents who were committed to justice first and secondly to Christian love were politically active and expected their minister to be politically involved. However, there were ministers following the ideals of liberation wished to be concerned with the development of a just social system and only secondarily were concerned with ritualism. In their vision they saw themselves as the guardians of justice and as such they assumed the right to be critical and challenge the actions of power figures. The prophets and later on the rabbis have always felt that they have a legitimate right

Justice: The illusive concept in Christian Theology

to see whether the people in power follow the political and moral ideals enumerated in the Mosaic teachings. Justice in the Jewish view is central to all relationships especially when such relationship is between the powerful and the powerless. For instance, in I Enoch (chapter 32-3) the powerful, i.e. the rich and the princess, are told that they will suffer when final judgment is rendered. Tzedek was so important in the Jewish value system that even God is bound to the principles of justice. God, therefore, could not be capricious in his judgments. Were He to use his power capriciously, the sufferers would be justified to indict God to a din-Torah to a rabbinical court where judgments are based on the Laws of the Torah. *(3) Given the paramount importance the prophets and the rabbinic leaders attributed to justice people's right to challenge and criticize the rulers of the land be they Jewish or not.

The ideal of justice was not incorporated in the early Christian canonical writings. Even a cursory view of the Concordance to the King James translation shows that the word justice as a noun does not appear in the New Testament. In the New Testament the Greek word dike, which most often is taken as the Greek equivalent of tzedek, the Hebrew term for justice, does not reflect the ideas encompassed in tzedek. Dike refers to righteousness,*(4) which is the result of having faith. An individual is said to be dikoi when one has faith in Christ which leads to receive the "free gift of grace" is unlike justice which proposes that grace is earned through action. Communal interaction and responsibility are, at most, by products of the grace-faith experience. God's relationship with his people is not an act based on justice but on righteousness in His faithfulness to the faithful. God's faithfulness in Greek is dikaosune Theo, is the view of God by which Paul justifies the rejection of the Torah law. (Rom.4:29 and Gal.3:25) Just as God's righteousness in his relationship with his faithful is a gift, that is the gift of salvation and redemption, so human righteousness is considered to be as an act of gift and as such it has the value of redemption. Paul thus introduces the essentiality of faith instead of action, as the

Faith and Conflict

core value of the new religion and with it justice the guiding norm of man-man and man-God relationship has been replaced by the value of love. It is love that brings salvation and not just action. The emphasis now is placed on righteousness through faith and gracious love (agape) – qualities that reside in the individual rather than justice (tzedek) that the system value of justice.

I need to point out again that the essence of the justice as expressed in the Jewish Bible has been used to be critical of the abuse of power. Those who exercise power, in this perspective, must be guided by normative constraints and their behavior must be held responsible for their behavior if they violate the moral norms. This right of criticism of power figures stands in direct opposition to that advocated by Paul whose view is that those in power need not justify nor defend their use of power. Accordingly Paul rejected the legitimacy of criticizing power figures and by de facto eliminated the importance of justice as a religious norm.

Why has Paul rejected tzedek? Why has Paul instead advocated the unconditional submission to Caesar as the legitimate symbol of worldly authority? In Judaism God even God Himself is bound by the norm of justice. Why did then Paul, a Jew, advocate the unquestioned submission to both God and Caesar?

I believe that we may gain a better understanding Paul's change from the Jewish political ideology to the one he advocated in the Christian Bible. This change to eliminate the subordinate's right to challenge the superordinate's power is Paul's attempt to accommodate Christianity and not challenge Roman power. In Paul's time Christianity was a new religion a numerical minority considered as a <u>supersticio</u>(superstition) and not as a <u>religio</u>. Perhaps it was Paul's view that subordinating Christianity to Roman authority would maximize Christianity's continued chance for existence. Accommodation and not confrontation permits the subordinate group to maintain its identity and existence. In order to do so, the subordinate group must eliminate from their values those ideals that may be perceived by the super-ordinate group as reflecting a hostile attitude toward them and advocate a value system that may be perceived as being a source for challenging the superordinate's group legitimacy to power.*(5) In short, a social system which finds itself in a subordinate position must adjust its ideology, often accepting advocating a submissive ideology so that its continued existence will be maximized. (For an in-depth discussion see K. Manheim Ideology and Utopia.)

In this paper I would like to propose that the elimination of tzedek as a central theme in the Christian Bible as an ideology and its substitution with agape and righteousness through faith may be seen as such a process. The elimination of tzedek removes the direct challenge to Rome's authority and power. At the same time the elevation of agape to both a moral dictum and an ideology also served an as an integrative force in the new Christian communities.

Most studies that have examined the new theology articulated by Paul have relied on textual analysis. I have no argument with the validity of hermeneutical analysis. I however, will examine this problem from a socio-historical perspective and shows how political conditions may have led to the new values of love have been incorporated as the central theme of Christian theology.

The two societies with which infant Christianity had to content with were Rome and Judea. This new religious movement, in order to maximize its existence, had to deal successfully with these two political entities. First, the leaders of Christianity, like all other peoples of that time in the Roman Empire, had to take cognizance of Rome's power and be aware of Rome's view of what they considered to be the political issues and political problems paramount to them. At the same time, Christians were also in a state of conflict with the Jews and their political and religious leaders. The latter centered on Christian claim that their new covenant with God is a legitimate one.

Faith and Conflict

Each social system, if it is to insure its survival, must reduce, if not completely eliminate, those conditions that are a threat to its continued existence. From this point of view, Christianity which came into existence during the most turbulent times in the Judean history (i.e. the Herodian and post Herodian period), had to contend with at least two problems. First, Christianity had to separate itself from Judaism and develop its own identity, and second, Christianity had to alter its image in the eyes of the ruling power. Their separation from Judaism was absolutely necessary in order to develop its own independent existence, if not as a new religion then at least as a new version that is to supplant the old religion. It had to have a new identity that would be perceived, at least by the Romans, as one different from and independent of Judaism. Secondly, and more important, that Christians unlike Jews reject the Jewish goals and values, especially their claims of seeking to make its country independent from Rome. Such a differentiation from the Jews was perceived by Paul as necessary to reduce existing Rome's extant hostility to Christians. In their encounter with the non-Jewish world, especially with Rome, Christians encountered both official and non-official hostility. Wilken (1948:18-20), for instance reports that Christians were accused both by the Romans and the non-Roman population of sacrificial murder, debauchery, killing children and drinking their blood, ritual intercourse, and eating the unborn child. In addition to the population's distrust, Christians also encountered official distrust. To Rome, religion was not a social institution that facilitated one's relationship with God, it was also a symbols of one's state and hence a political institution.

In order to assure Rome's welfare and its protection it was required that the inhabitants worship Rome's God. The continual existence of Rome was considered to be tied directly with the continued existence and the worship of the Roman gods. Cicero's attack of Catalina was motivated by the latter's rejection of the Roman gods. Such a rejection was not necessarily a blasphemy but it was considered the act of a traitor of Rome. Cicero comments in the De Nature Deorum (The Nature of the Gods) that in all probability the disappearance of piety towards the gods will entail the disappearance of loyalty and social union among men as well [as well as] justice itself the queen of all virtues (Yonge, 1892).

In spite of the fact that Jews have enjoyed a degree of freedom in Rome, nonetheless Rome had a particular distrust of the Jewish religion and the associated politics. Jews had been one of the staunchest opponents to Roman rule and fought against assimilation into the Roman way of life. Hadrian was among the most ruthless attacker of Jews. The tension between Rome and the Jews is evident in the writing of Tacitus. He comments that Moses led the Jews out of Egypt and established a new religion which is quite different from those of the rest of mankind. Wilken (1983:39-40) quotes Tacitus: Among Jews all things are profane that we hold sacred; on the other hand they regard permissible what to us seems immoral. They prohibit the eating of pork, fast often, celebrate a meal with unleavened bread, and sit idle one day out of each week. Their practices are sinister and revolting. The Jews are wicked, given to lust, and look on other men and women as enemies. They even introduce the practice of circumcision to show that they are different from others. Their proselytes despise the god of the Romans and eventually shed their patriotism to Rome. In short they are most criminal people.

The view that Jews were politically dangerous was pervasive among the Romans in the time of Christ, and the formation of religious cults that were many in Judea was seen to be the formation of political opposition. The purported inscription on the cross on which Jesus was crucified INRI (the abbreviation of Jesus of Nazareth King of the Jews) attests the Roman view of Christians as a political entity. It seems reasonable, therefore, to assume that in the face of Rome's hostility to non-Roman religions in general and to the Jewish one in particular, Christian leadership would attempt to separate itself from Judaism and

Faith and Conflict

thereby indicate to Rome that this new religion was not political and unlike the Jewish sects the Pharisees and the Sadducees it does not seek political ends. In so doing Christian leaders may have hoped to reduce Rome's opposition to Christianity and thus alleviate a threat to its existence. Rome's threat to the Christian existence was greater that its threat to the continued Jewish existence. Unlike Christians, Jews continued to live in their historical land and continued to maintain a high degree of local hegemony over the population. The Sanhedrin, the high religious court was still functioning and interpreting the laws of the country.

How could this new religious movement indicate to Rome its non-political nature? It was done by separating themselves from the Jews, creating a new identity and by a symbolic declaration of their submission to the ruling power. The acquisition of a new identity has two features. First, it consists of a declaration of what the new group is and what it stands for, that is, an existential declaration. Second, it includes a dialectical statement relative to the old group from which it has arisen, that is, a clear juxtaposition to the older group from which it has arisen (see Coser, 1956). With regard to the first, Christians declared themselves to have a new covenant based on faith. Since the new faith, at least in the beginning, was not markedly different from the older one, their dialectical juxtaposition from Judaism was even more important. After all, there were many synagogues in Judea under the leadership of James who remained in essence Jewish, but who also accepted Jesus as their savior. It is in this regard that Paul reinforced the idea that this new religion is faith and not action centered. The most significant symbol of their separation from Judaism came with Paul's rejection of two sine qua non features in the Jewish religion: the law and circumcision. These two elements of the Jewish religion served as their sign both to themselves and to others of their particularistic association to God and their nationhood. By rejecting the law, Christian also rejected the "contractual" nature of religion with its emphasis on deeds based

Justice: The illusive concept in Christian Theology

on the Jews' declaration at Sinai "we shall do and we shall listen." A faith orientated religion, unlike a contractual law and deeds based religion, assumes that a person in power, because of low, empathy and unselfishness, will not exploit his position.* (6) An emphasis on faith and on trust requires little or no proof by action. While in Judaism God sits in judgment and examines people's deeds in Christianity he only seeks proof of faith. Justice that is central to the Jewish religion requires proof of a person's adherence to a norm guided behavior. In early Christianity, and to some extent even today, an emphasis on faith requires little or no proof of normative action. Central to Christianity is the belief that righteousness is achieved through faith alone, and it is faith and not action that is rewarded by achieving the state of grace. Salvation is attained through grace rather than works (see Kittel, 1966, Vol.X:210)*7 (Because of the emphasis on faith some theologians, like Luther, found the teaching of James problematic.) In short, the elimination of judgment on action makes the idea of justice theoretically and logically superfluous.

A second reason for minimizing the Christian concern for justice as a system property and substituting the concern for righteousness of the individual, I propose, is that in this manner Christians sought to reduce Roman hostility against them. In ancient Judaism, justice was associated with power and criticism. In the name of justice both prophets and charismatic leaders (including Jesus) claimed the right to be critical of the political and economic leaders' action. Otherwise, Jesus would have not believed to have the right to be critical of and especially punitive to the money lenders. After all, a contractual relationship, which was the core of Judaic perception of interpersonal relationship both with God and with earthly power figures, is judged by the action of the parties. Such a judgment is no longer necessary when contractual nature of the relationship is eliminated. Power and its exercise thereof in Christianity was considered legitimate in its own right and became independent of religious concern – that is, one had to render Caesar that which is

Faith and Conflict

Caesar's,*(8) and God became separated from the human world and the political action therein. In Judaic tradition, both God and those in power must abide by specific ethics which govern the relationship among parties of unequal power. In the Christian Bible God's power assumes a new dimension. Unlike the description of God in the Jewish Bible, the Christian view holds that both God and Christ's power is now directed to save the Christian community from Satan and loss of salvation. In short the issue of God's power is no longer seen as an essential element in interpersonal relationships (Kittel, 1966, Vol. II., 298) Thus, by eliminating both justice and power as religious issues, Christian leaders indicated to Rome that Christians were no longer concerned with the political power issue because their religion has placed its fundamental purpose to other-worldly concerns of salvation.

But why has the issue of justice become so central in the Jewish religion? Of course, the emphasis on justice, like other values arise out of existential concerns of a society. It does not necessarily as Marx has argued reflect the interests of those in the ruling power. Nor does it have to be the result of a dialectical relationship that maintained a common belief system. In the Jewish instance I would like to propose that the concern for justice was a natural response to the organizational structure of the tribal association of the Children of Israel. The Jewish state began as a confederation of tribes. The unity of this confederation was achieved by the centralization of worship revolving first around the Tabernacle in Shiloh and then the Temple in Jerusalem and secondly was the covenantal relationship of the tribes. In this confederation of tribes that was called Israel each tribe was economically and politically independent. There was however the covenant specifying each tribe's duties to the other specifying their mutual obligation for purposes defense. In Chapter 32 in the Book of Numbers the Gadites and Reubenites petitioned Moses that they would like to settle in Trans-Jordan since it was cattle country. Moses rebuked them for he thought that they will violate the covenant in which each tribe swore to fulfill their duty in the war to make Canaan the land of Israel. To which the Gadites and Reubenites responded that they will leave their cattle, children and women on the other side of the Jordan but they will hasten as shock-troops and stay to fulfill their duty till the whole land is conquered. So the two and half tribes Gad, Reuben and the half tribe of Manasseh settled to the east of the Jordan. Perhaps the one of the most significant infra-structure of the early Jews was the covenant that they had with God. As I see it, the significant covenant was one between the tribes. To assure its continued importance the covenant between the tribes has become a part of the Jews covenant with God. Thus Moses spoke to the two tribes that they cannot abandon their duty for such an act constitutes the violation of the covenant with God. By equating these two covenants the tribal covenant has assumed sanctity. In the book of Judges (Chapter 4) Barak who was leading the army of the tribe of Ephraim to free them from the rule of Jabin the king of Canaan sent messengers to the other tribes to remind them of that they must come to their aid as it was specified in the covenant.

The covenant is a form of a contract, one sanctified by God. The essential feature of a contract is the agreement of quid pro quo a just agreement between two or more parties. No covenant can exist without the idea that justice must be maintained, that the violation by any one party of the agreement is performing an unjust deed. Of course once the principle of justice has become a central norm in a society its application is incorporated to all forms of covenants and contracts. Durkheim (1984 p.162) espouses one important feature of the Jewish conception of a contract, a view that differs from that which is prevalent in this country. According to our view a contract when signed, regardless whether fair or not, is a binding contract. In contrast Durkheim who sees contracts as forms of covenants states: Agreements between parties cannot make a clause fair which of itself is unfair. There are rules of justice that social justice must prevent being violated, even if a clause has been agreed by the parties concerned". If a set of values is to become

Faith and Conflict

important to members of a society, it needs not only to address itself (or appear to address itself) to the physical and cultural survival of the members, but it also cannot prescribe ends that are unattainable by the members of the society. Social values that demand values that are unattainable and which do not reflect the interests of the members of society's social conditions become dysfunctional.*(9) Such conditions will increase alienation and anomie and will not enhance social integration, to the contrary as Merton (1968) pointed out it becomes a source of social tension. Thus, if Christianity would have retained justice as its central concern it would have made it difficult if not impossible for Christian communities to exist.

The underlying reason for this thesis is to be found in the Jewish and Christian class differences during the first century A.D., particularly during Paul's life time. Jews, after having taken over the land from the Canaanites and having created the states of Israel and Judea both in the pre and post exilic period, were most often politically independent, and with it they enjoyed a degree of self-determination. Judaism in this political state was, like all other religions in that era, a national-political religion. It is because it was a theocratic state that the prophets and other charismatic leaders enjoyed political status and power. In later years there was a triumvirate of political ruling classes. Members that were part of the Keter Torah consisting of the rabbis, like for instance Rabbi Akivah, Ben Zoma and many others shared power with the kings and princess Keter Malchuth, and the High Priest and the Temple priests that made up the Keter Kehunah. Because of Torah that served as the Jewish constitution the Prophets and later the Rabbis in the name of YAHVEH could legitimately demand justice – that is, an accounting from and be critical of the ruling class' those who constituted the keter Torah's action. Although the Jews lost this constitutional privilege during the Roman rule Christians never developed it in the first place. The Christians were not in a position to be concerned with justice for they never had nor could they develop and justify a perspective which in their view gave them the right to demand accounting from the rulers. The Sanhedrin i.e. the court of the seventy even during the Roman times demanded accounting from the local officials and even the Roman governor consulted them. Unlike the Jews, members of the new Christian sects consisted primarily of slaves, ex-slaves, and lower class artisans – the powerless classes. If justice leads to or is associated with people's right to demand accounting otherwise leading to rebellion then what kind of value will develop among the powerless? Manheim(1936:196) suggests that in the face of power and its ideology the powerless develop a utopian weltanschauung. Manheim writes: "It is clear that those social strata which represent the prevailing social and intellectual order will experience as reality that structure of relationship of which they are the bearers, while the groups driven into opposition to the present order will be oriented towards the first stirrings of the social order for which they are striving and which is being realized through them."

The ideas and beliefs that arise in the subjugated group stand in a dialectical relationship to those of the ruling group. In short the new ideas are the negation of the ruling class ideology. Mannheim for instance points as an example of such negation the Christian view expressed in the Bible "The last shall be first" as a dialectical view to the ruling class. In this case, for example, one could say in the case of Christianity, it was resentment which gave the lower strata courage to emancipate themselves, at least physically, from the domination of an unjust system of values and to set up their own opposition to it . . . (1936:25) The new and opposing values were not, he continues addressed to men in general, but rather that it has a real appeal only those who, like the Christians, are in some manner oppressed and who, at the same time, under the impulse of resentment, wished to free themselves from prevailing injustices (1936:25)

The early Christians' lower social and economic status and lack of power led them to reject the idea of seeking justice (which is the

Faith and Conflict

prerogative of those who have at least some power by virtue of economic control or at least in their large population) and instead elevate a value that stresses the importance of emotion and commitment i.e., love and agape. For a people who lack power, any norm or value which justifies the demands for and the exercise of justice can only lead to increased frustration. I would like to propose the following analogy. If I were to visit one who is dying of cancer, and for which disease there is no cure, what can I offer the dying person? The inflicted one cannot demand from me that I cure him. All I can do is to give him hope for a better future world and love. The frustration that Christians must have experienced due to their powerlessness and negative view that the population held of them could only be addressed through the transvaluation of values, that is by altering the importance of values. Transvaluation of values occurs when a subjugated and powerless group alters the values of the dominant class and advocates the opposite values. For instance instead of focusing on the importance of this world the transvaluated values stress the primacy of life in the other world or the value of being poor and a world where the meek will eventually inherit the world. In short such values do not represent a political ideology but a utopian vision. The idea of retribution and taking vengeance for the wrongs endured and the demand for justice and judgment has been transferred to the deity. In this world, instead of justice as a guide for interpersonal relationships, the ideal of communal love (agape) has been substituted. Thus, for people who lack the power to control their own fate and who see themselves void of power, interpersonal relationships will be guided by the value of love. This value is not extended to all people but to those who are members of the shared faith.

Of course the Christian's subjugation and powerlessness lasted only until 350 C.E. when Constantine made Christianity the state religion. Still, the founding values have remained most often only per forma. In contrast because of the value of justice remained central to the Jewish value system even when they lived subjugated in their Diaspora of

Justice: The illusive concept in Christian Theology

two millennia instead of developing a utopian value of love Jews have organized mutual help societies. Such mutual help societies reflected the ideal of Tzedokoh i.e. charity but one that is based on tzedek on the principle of justice that meant the legitimate right of the needy to receive communal help.

The legacy that resulted from the socio-political condition of early Christians that led to their emphasis on agape and the minimization of justice has led to a political perspective that was supported by the Christian church. The most important ideology is a conservative political orientation coupled with an opposition to social change. It is for this reason that liberal theologian are seeking ways by which the Christian ideal could be given new meaning and interpretation so that it could be used to legitimate their quest for social justice. One such re-interpretation is Niebuhr's view that justice is but love in action. But as Paul clearly points out in his letter to the Galatians, the law (and also justice) is only needed by people committed to the way of flesh, while faith and love alleviate the necessity for justice. The discrepancy between a commitment to justice and to love is also evident in that the former sees that the right to be critical of power is the legitimate right of all members of one's community; the latter is associated with submission to power and instead of criticism, or at least as Paul states, emphasis should be placed to develop the qualities of long suffering, gentleness, goodness, temperance, and meekness. These are the qualities that are associated with heavenly rewards. Thus, the final question still remains: Given the commitment to love and the absence of justice as a fundamental value, can Christian theology support social change, particularly when such change is required for the society's well being and needs the alteration of theological perspective and which also calls into question the values espoused by the power elite?

The absence of the New Testament's commitment to justice is evident in a number of ways. Justice, for instance, is not included among the 20 most important terminal values in Rokeach's (1979) study.

Faith and Conflict

Rokeach asked 100 respondents to enumerate the values that they considered important —justice was not mentioned. Dean M. Kelly, a theologian, proposes that while justice has been a very important in the Jewish tradition as exemplified in the writings of the prophets in the Old Testament, in the Christian tradition the idea of justice with the additional value of love. Yet, at the end of his analysis of justice, Kelley concludes that despite the Hebraic tradition, justice is not and cannot be a part of religion. Justice, he argues, is a utilitarian end and "[A]nything as elemental —as visceral—as religion is not going to be 'pressed into service' to attain any utilitarian ends" He then concludes his article by stating that"[A]lthough Christian and Jews have a duty to pursue justice, it is not the goal or justification of religion."(1984:9). The pursuit of justice Kelley proposes, arises out of a more primary need and that is to pursue love. But as he sees it justice is not a part of Christian theology.

The legacy inherited from the socio-political conditions that led to an emphasis on agape and minimization of justice has important consequences for society. First, Christian theology limits religious morality to personal morality, namely what the individual does, but it does not emphasize or makes morality problematic in the action pursued by those in political power. Such a definition would legitimate the criticism of those in power that is contrary to the teaching of Paul. For this reason liberation theology has failed to gain legitimacy and the support from the public at large or from the church leaders. Second, justice is the moral imperative which is central to moral integration and the quality that is an essential feature of advanced societies. Hence Durkheim declares that today "justice must prevail." *(10)

Notes:

1. This is a revised version of a paper published in the Review of Religious Research (1989) Vol.30:236-243.
2. For an in-depth discussion of justice see Rawls, 1971. The difficulty of defining justice because of its complexity is well argued by Voight and Thornton 1984. For this reason we limited our analysis of justice as it is used in the Jewish Bible.
3. This theme can be found in the Agadoth (rabbinic tales and legends) as well as among the Chassidic tales. Philo of Alexandria (a Jewish philosopher) points out that both God and those in power are to govern by ethical traits. On this basis Philo argues that power has specific ethical foundations. (See Kittel Vol.II p.298)
4. I am distinguishing justice, a norm and a property of a social system in contrast to righteousness a quality that defines an individual. Societies can be describes as being just that is that its norms and laws are based of the principles of justice as opposed to an individual quality, that is a part of his character.
5. Habermas for instance, points out that in traditional societies crisis occurs when the validity claims of the system's norms and justification which have permitted exploitation are challenged. This crisis is solved through the actual production of new validity claims. (Habermas 1975:20)
6. There is an implicit faith that a good Christian ruler will obey the law of "love" and will therefore act kindly to his subjects. This type of governing as Kant has observed, exercises the greatest conceivable acts of despotism. (Kant 1973:106-7)
7. Justice, in the Jewish conception is necessary for the maintenance of a good quality of life in this world and also carries with it rewards in the world to come. After death each person's soul stands 121 in

judgment before God, the Judge, who examines whether one has exercised appropriate justice in his lifetime. (Jewish legends)
8. The importance of adherence to temporal power, so long as it is just, has been advocated by the rabbis of the first century. The Talmud states dina d' malchutah dina i.e. the law of the land is the law.
9. In his analysis of suicide Durkheim (1951) argues that to seek ends that are unattainable is to condemn oneself to a perpetual state of unhappiness. 10. Durkheim's view of the importance of justice is well advanced by Sirianni (1984).

References:

1. Apocrypha, The –The Book of Enoch in the Old Testament, 1959, New York: Vintage Books
2. Coser, L.A., 1956, The Functions of Social Conflict. Glencoe IL. The Free Press
3. Durkheim, Emile, 1966, Suicide New York, The Free Press.
4. Ibid., 1984, The Division of Labor in Society. New York, The Free Press
5. Kant, I., 1973, Two Essays on Right in Economic Justice. Baltimore MD. Penguin
6. Kelley, Dean "Religion and Justice: the volcano and the terrace." In Review of Religious, 1984, Research 26:3-14
7. Kittel, Gerhard 1966, Theoretical Dictionary of the New Testament, Grand Rapids, MIch: Eerdmans.
8. Lewy, Guenther 1974, Religion and Revolution. New York: Oxford University Press 122

Christianity and the Geo-Political Conditions:

9. Manheim, Karl 1936, Ideology and Utopia. New York: Harcourt, Brace
10. Niebuhr, H.R. 1995, Social Sources of Denominationalism. University of Virginia Press.
11. Rawls, John 1971, Theory of Justice. Cambridge: Harvard University Press
12. Rokeach, Milton 1979, Understanding Human Values: Individual and Social. New York: The Free Press
13. Schoenfeld, Eugen 1974, Love and Justice: the effect of religious values on liberalism and conservatism. Review of Religious Research 6:41-46
14. Sirianni, Carmen J. 1984, "Justice and then division of labor: a reconsideration of Durkheim's Division of Labor in Society." Sociological Review 32:449-470
15. Voight, Lydia and W.E. Thornton 1984, Limits of Justice: A Sociological Analysis, New York: University, Press of America.
16. Wilken, Robert L. 1984, The Christians as the Romans Saw Them. Yale University Press 17. Yongue, C.D. 1982, The Treatises of M.T. Cicero. London: George Bell 123

Section IV: Solution to the Problem

Introduction to Section IV

Some years ago I attended a meeting at which one of the speakers was a teacher of history at a Catholic High School. Among the subjects he taught was also the history of the Holocaust. In his lecture he told us, an audience of predominantly survivors, what he considers to be the impelling view of the significance of the Holocaust and why it is taught in his High School. Of course the dominant reason was to teach the value of tolerance as means of enhancing the students moral development and inculcating the ideals virtue into their character. However there were other reasons. It seems, the speaker admitted, that by teaching the Holocaust the Church hoped to make amends for its failure to protest the genocide as being immoral and contrary to the church's ideals. Moreover, teaching about the Holocaust may help to alter Catholic teaching about Jews that in at least in his view, may have inadvertently contributed to the problems that the European Jews experienced in the last two millennia. During the Q&A I asked the speaker: If indeed the root of Anti-Semitism in the Christian world lies in the Bible than wouldn't it be reasonable that the Church would at least present a reinterpretation of these descriptions? Of course I could not expect that the offending passages in the Bible would be

Faith and Conflict

eliminated. After all it is a book that is holy and error free to many billions of believers. But I have hoped that a reinterpretation of the text is definitely warranted. Of course, being a devout Catholic the teacher could not agree with my suggestion. The best solution he could propose was, and it is what he teaches, is to inculcate in the students a sense of tolerance of other faiths. Tolerance for a long time was the buzz word, the sine qua non for the development of a peaceful society. In this section I point out the idea of tolerance tends, <u>sub rosa</u>, to justify intolerance and I conclude that while tolerance may enhance the interpersonal relationships among some people it does not have the force to eliminate hostile behavior towards subordinate minority groups. If tolerance, like the teaching of love, especially to love one's enemy has never had a positive on inter-religious relationship how will the teaching of tolerance will reduce hostilities? The answer, at least in my view it will not. There are many persons, especially who advocate

The ideologies of the extreme right like Glenn Beck who declared that one should run away from those churches that teach the importance of social and economic justice but instead teach personal tolerance, we will, as the right seeks, maintain the <u>status quo </u>ante and intolerance will continue to rule the land. Contrary to, if we seek greater harmony, we must increase the teaching and make social justice the foundation of this country's philosophy.

The principle of tolerance of others and of love that have arisen in homogeneous societies are functional in a homogeneous society only. However, in a heterogeneous society composed of a diversity of, religions, ethnic and racial groups only the ascendancy of the moral principle of justice can reduce inter group hostility.

In the two essays contained in this section I elaborate on the principles of tolerance and justice.

The Fallacy of Tolerance

As a survivor of the Holocaust, one of the greatest legally instituted intolerances and genocide, I have hoped that we in the United States could devote time and effort to find an antidote for that social cancer that has infected many societies. In the wake of black and women's revolution it was proposed by many that if people would become tolerant of diversity we could achieve social harmony. I too, like so many, have succumbed to the view that was espoused both in academia and churches proposing that to achieve a harmonious society we need to inculcate an attitude of tolerance toward others who differ from the majority, whose culture is different from the majority's, whose body color differs, and those whose god or gods differ from the majority's view.. I believed that if religions would indoctrinate their adherents and if public schools would socialize their students to accept and abide by the principle of tolerance then tolerance would act as a prophylaxis against anti-Semitism that in Germany has led to the Holocaust. In fact tolerance became the "buzz-word" advocated by ministers, social workers, and teachers and assumed the mantle of being the magic bullet that would destroy inter racial, religious and ethnic hostility.

Yet, with time, I became aware that our idea is flawed. I soon realized that although tolerance is a desirable virtue (in contrast to a moral authority) and it may even positively influence some people's relationship with members of other races and religions, it will not, on its own change individual perspectives and the social conditions that most often are the root causes of intra and inter societal hostilities.

Even a cursory examination of the definition of tolerance will show that tolerance proposes that the people or things that we are asked to tolerate are inherently inferior. In fact, contrary to the intended purpose as a producer of social harmony, the word tolerance creates, reinforces, and legitimates a form of social differentiation that declares some

Faith and Conflict

people to be superior and others inferior a view that led to the existence of social disharmony in the first place.

The meaning of the word tolerance proposes, perhaps indirectly, a view that the minorities whom we are asked to tolerate are undesirable. Consider the dictionary definition of tolerance which defines It: the capacity to endure. We use the word tolerance to indicate that under certain conditions we need, or, rather we must endure certain unavoidable and undesirable events or conditions. For instance, under certain circumstances we must learn to tolerate pain. Or, we must learn to tolerate certain unfavorable environmental factors such as pollution because we cannot alter these undesirable conditions. Similarly, we are told that we must learn to tolerate and accept diverse human beings even when they may be considered by us as undesirable. We are asked to tolerate them not only because they are a part of life and quite often perform a necessary and important function for society. But, more importantly, we in this Christian society are asked to be tolerant for it is the fulfillment of the Christian dicta to love one's neighbor. We are asked in the name of Christian love to endure these undesirable persons.

This perspective is similar to my mother's reasoning when I, as a young boy, fought with my younger brother. "Tuli" she would say, "you are the older one and you have more sense. Give in to your brother. Be tolerant of him." She appealed to my ego and defining me as the older and hence smarter than my brother hence it is up to me to be tolerant of him.

By accepting the value of being tolerant of others who are not only Unlike us but in most instances inferior to us we do not redefine their character or their desirability. We do not describe them as being equal to and perhaps in some manner even superior to us because in order that we become tolerant we must admit that the people whom we will tolerate are inherently undesirable otherwise the idea of tolerance makes no sense.

Similarly, those who are being tolerated are also asked to be tolerant of the discriminators and those who seek to harm those who to discriminate and harm us. The request for tolerating the enemy is justified by the Christian teaching of turning the other cheek. The sufferers, the mistreated, and the abused are taught to be tolerant of their tormentors because they are told that such suffering is a virtue and the exercise of this virtue will lead to rewards in the world to come. The famous statement by Jesus "Father forgive them for they know not what they do" is an example of an ideology that tells the sufferers that it is a virtue to tolerate their tormentors. By forgiving the tormentors the sufferers become the better persons and spiritually more advanced and most importantly that by tolerating and loving the enemy they will be assured of a better life in heaven. After all, it is far more difficult for the rich to receive salvation than for the camel to pass through the eye of a needle. Gary Marx, in his study, of black minister's attitude to Martin Luther King found that those who believed and advocated the primacy of religious salvation were less likely to support the civil right movement's demand for justice and social change than those who placed primacy to this worldly life. (Karl, Mannheim 1955 and Gary T. Marx 1967)

If I and other Jews, and for that matter all minorities, are to be tolerated by the majority who hold power in society then, by the very definition of the term, I must consider myself, as a Jew, an undesirable although an inevitable part in the lives of the majority. Members of the majority, the powerful majority, may not like the minorities in this country but, we, the minority groups, are asked by the majority to develop the virtue of tolerance toward us. In short minorities are asked to develop what Mannheim calls a utopian ideology.

Are the American Jews or other minorities an inevitable pain or natural calamity that the majority must learn to endure? Notice that it is the minorities who are asking the majority for tolerance, and, not vice versa. Members of the majority do not seek or request to be tolerated.

Faith and Conflict

Instead they demand justice, freedom, and the social conditions that they consider to be their inalienable rights. Should not minorities also expect these self-same privileges? Should not the minorities too, be given the same rights that are demanded by the majority?

The inequitable relationship between lower and higher classes, between those who tolerate and those being tolerated is described by Aristotle. Living in Athens in a highly stratified society he proposed that only the gentlemen of high social status posses the quality of virtue. Only they have the capacity for magnanimity and munificence. This is similar to the medieval notion inherent in the virtue of noblesse oblige that proposes that those in power and who possess wealth should as a matter of Christian charity and their greater moral sensitivity exercise tolerance toward those in the lower rungs of society. Privilege it is proposed carries with it this burden. This is the duty and the burden of the privileged that they must develop in themselves the virtues of magnanimity and munificence and be helpful to and be tolerant of the lower classes. When in trouble, the lower rungs of the social stratum can appeal to those in the upper stratum that they, because of their social status, should be tolerant and should therefore grant the underprivileged the favor to be left alone and the right to exist. Traditionally, the lower classes never demanded their rights. They merely entreat the super-ordinate classes who have the power and control over them that they, the possessors of virtues and character, should also have a sense of fairness when relating to them. The sub-ordinate class' relationship with the super-ordinate is modeled on the manner that religion instructs us to relate to God. In Judaism, for instance, prior to petitioning God for his mercies people recite the thirteen attributes of God (Exodus 34:6-7) and remind Him that He as the possessor of all the good attributes He should deal kindly with the petitioner. Whether we follow Judaism, Christianity, or Islam we never place demands on God we always petition Him. Thus, if we propose that relationships between social strata should be governed by tolerance then we also provide the ideology by which we legitimate the continual existence of power and privilege differences. In short, tolerance does not alter the social conditions that made tolerance necessary in the first place.

Let us look at another aspect of tolerance, namely that those who ask for tolerance must pay for the privilege of being tolerated. The price the tolerated pay is contained in the norm of reciprocity that proposes that those who ask for tolerance must also be submissive to those who are superior in the social stratum. Submissiveness especially combined with gratitude to those of superior power develops in the lower classes meekness which bars the members of the inferior classes to challenge the legitimacy of the power inherent in the superior classes. The price the minorities must pay for being tolerated is to abstain from being critical of the majority. For Jews that meant that they cannot be critical of and fault Christians for not only for their beliefs that have advocated intolerance of Jews but, also for the societal laws that are founded on Christian beliefs and theology. Sunday laws have always been imposed on all people, for believers and non believers alike. Similarly Christmas was considered a holiday and it became binding on every one. Any criticism that challenged the right of the Christian majority to impose its values as laws was considered as lacking the sense of gratitude that minorities should have for the privilege of having the right to exist is this "free" country.

I was told of a repartee between Alan Derschowitz the noted lawyer and Pat Robertson a former candidate for the Presidency and founder of the Christian Network regarding the legitimacy of having Christian prayers in the public schools classes. Derschowitz opposed class room prayer. In his view this violates the constitution that imposes separation of church and state. He suggested to Robertson that those who wish to pray should be given access to a room in which prayers could be offered before classes start. Reverend Robertson opposed this view. Instead, he proposed that those who do not wish to participate in prayers should leave the class room. In his view Christians have the right to offer

Faith and Conflict

prayers in the classroom "after all" he argued "we were here first." This exemplifies the majority view that minorities should be grateful for the tolerance and freedom that they are granted.*

The demand for submission to and being non critical of the majority became evident to me in another way. After arriving to the United States I was often asked "How do you like America?" In the beginning I was not aware that this question was merely a rhetorical one similar to the question "How are you?" When one is asked about the state of his health one should be aware that it is merely a courtesy question for which the standard response is "OK." Very few, if any at all, of the questioners wish to hear a lengthy response about the others state of health. Similarly when I was asked about my view of the U.S no one really wished for me to tell them what I really thought. The expected response to the question was "I like it very much." After all I was a tolerated immigrant and as such I must indicate my respect and adoration of my new homeland. But due to my ignorance I thought that those who asked me were genuinely interested in my answer I proceeded to expound my views. So long as I was complementary of the US the questioner was polite and feigned interest. However, when I became somewhat critical of the U.S. his (or her) response was immediate and harsh. Most often it came as the following abhor "Well, if you don't like it here why don't you go back where you came from." As a foreigner I was tolerated only if I do not challenge any aspect of my host country's superiority over all other countries.

This price for being tolerated was strongly evident when I visited Oxford in England. I commented to Jewish professors while attending synagogue services that during my two month stay there I never encountered any public criticisms by Jews against England's negative policies towards Israel. Their response was "we do not dare." In short they felt that Jews in England are still viewed as tolerated strangers and if the Jews in England were to criticize English policies their freedom to exist as Jews would be in danger. Of course, Jews in England have in the past encountered official anti-Semitism. They were not only expelled from the country but have also experienced a number of massacres.

An additional problem with tolerance is that by instilling this value into the individual we will as a consequence improve society and the social system. There is a prevalent, albeit an erroneous assumption that guides our politics is that the way to improve society is through improving the individuals that constitute society. This perspective is related to our view of society. Most people believe that society is not an entity in its own right, as Durkheim referred to as being "sui generic." Rather, people define society merely as the sum of the individuals in it. This perspective leads most Americans to believe that if we would improve the quality of the individuals that constitute the society it will, ipso facto, improve society itself. Perhaps a most extreme example of this point of view is reflected in Lester Maddox's former governor of Georgia view of how to improve the prison system. In his view if we were to get a better quality of prisoners the system would improve by itself. In short, if we would improve the character of the people who compose this country, that is, if we but inculcate into children the need to love our neighbors and to be tolerant of their differences we would improve the quality of interpersonal relationships. This point of view is unfortunately, not valid. Society and the individuals in it are two separate entities. Society and the individuals in it do not have a reciprocal relationship and hence individuals have little impact on the nature and character of society. To the contrary, it is society that molds and shapes the character and nature of the individual. **

I have already pointed out that individualism is one and perhaps most fundamental value orientation in this society. Max Weber and others have argued that it is the secularized Protestant value that led to the rise of individualism and simultaneously to an opposition to collectivism. Weber argued that it is the rise of secular individualism that was the foundation on which capitalism and modernity rests. In this

Faith and Conflict

ethos of individualism MacIntyre (1984) proposes "each of us is taught to see himself or herself as an autonomous moral agent; but each of us also becomes engaged by modes of practice, aesthetic or bureaucratic, which involve us in manipulative relationships with others."(68) In such an ethos the impact of collective moral perspective on the individual has waned. McIntyre suggests that what is needed today is the re-introduction of personal virtues. His view is that in most modern societies the individual is isolated from society's rule and the individual becomes an entity all by himself and to himself.

While on the one hand individualism as an ideology, helped the rise of capitalism And also to free ourselves from society's impact and from the yoke imposed by the church and monarchies but on the other hand the newly acquired personal freedom leaves the individuals to their own devices without any powerful force to guide them or constrain them from egoism and associated excesses. Under such condition there is a rise in suicide rates (Durkheim 1951) and quite frequently they are also subject to fear of the future that often results in rage.(Fromm 1994) Only submission to social morals based on justice and not the possession of individual virtues that can provide societal stability.

Another reason why we in the United States have elevated tolerance as a moral virtue and designated it as the sine qua non for the making of a harmonious society is our faith in the efficacy of the Christian teaching of love. However, it should be quite evident that this religious teaching in the last two millennia has improved neither the individual nor society or the nature of human relationships in societies. How often have we heard that white slave owners quite often had great affection for their slaves? Such affections to "mammies" for instance did not change the nature of superordinate and subordinate relationships nor the customs, traditions, and the laws that governed owner and slave relations.

The Christian principle of love presupposes that we must exercise charity and benevolence to all. The principle of love as a guide for human relationships as I proposed in my other essays (included in this book and elsewhere) is fraught with many problems. Most importantly, love does not address itself to the issue of rights. Inequitable treatment and the justification for differential access to life's chances do not violate the principle of Christian love. Love, does not raise a critical question whether differential treatment and quality of life associated with social positions in a stratified society is justifiable. Love, I propose, is the ideology that laid the foundation for the development of the medieval ethic of noblesse oblige, the laissez faire ethic of early capitalism, and the benevolent ethic of the latter nineteenth and the twentieth century.

Let me comment briefly on the benevolent ethic that I believe still dominates our perception of what should guide human relationships in a stratified society. Fundamentally the benevolent ethic proposes that social classes have a moral covenant with members of inferior classes. Bendix (1956) quotes Malthus who proposes that "the higher classes need to meet their responsibilities effectively and enable the "lower classes" to mitigate their distress to the extent that this was within the power of man."(Bendix p.79) In this moral view of inter-class relationship, Bendix reports, the upper classes have a responsibility toward the lower classes in the same manner as the Devine Providence has a responsibility to the well being of the higher classes. Malthus transformed Burke's earlier writing in this regard. He proposes that the upper and middle classes need to improve "the conditions of the poor; to show them what they can and what they cannot do; and that, although much may be done by advice and instruction, by encouraging habits of prudence and cleanliness, by discriminate charity, and by any mode of bettering the present condition of the poor… (Quoted in Bendix 1956 p. 80)

The duties that the upper classes have towards the lower classes are contingent upon the duties of the lower classes to listen to and comply with the advice given to them by the superior classes. Charitable help that is given by the superior classes to the lower ones has always assumed the character of a gift. However, the person who is the recipient of a gift

Faith and Conflict

becomes beholden to the giver till the receiver can reciprocate with a gift of equal value. In this manner those who possess greater wealth can exercise personal charity and in this manner make the recipients remain subservient to the giver. It is this relationship upon which benevolent ethic is founded. (See Marcel Mauss 1923)

I must now consider another problem associated with tolerance as a social value and a moral guide for inter-group relationships and is it's similarity to cultural relativism. Those who follow the relativist perspective propose that we cannot judge the morals of ethnic, racial, or religious groups by the same standard. Different societies they argue, respond to social reality in different manner and hence their moral and ethical values will develop relative to the conditions in which they exist. For instance, societies that live in areas that have scarce resources will emphasize the importance of competition, a value that reflects existing competition of scarce resources i.e. food necessary for existence. Of course many people see the world from this perspective and declare morality must accept the reality of <u>bellum omnia contra omnes</u>. On the other hand, societies where food can be gained only by common effort the emphasis will be on collectivism. For instance the plains Indians whose main sustenance was derived from hunting the Buffalo had to develop a value of cooperation. This point of view led to the idea that we must tolerate differences because the values that motivate behavior differ from group to group. This perspective is inherent in the social philosophy that stresses the idea of laissez faire laissez passé. Live and let live and let each person have the freedom to live as one pleases. This perspective then proposes that people representing different cultures must be given total freedom of speech and action. We must be tolerant of diversity.

But, must we tolerate all diversities in the same manner that we must tolerate diversities of thought and speech? This question has not been problematic to those who advocate tolerance. The anti-Kohlbergians and I was one in my younger years, advocating moral relativism would argue that we should tolerate all diversities even though some of their values may oppose values that we hold dear to us. The question is never raised: Are there any occasions when we should be intolerant of teachings that not only stand in a diametric opposition to ours but deny the values that we consider fundamental to a just civil society? Such was the question that Oliver Wendell Holmes faced by inquiring whether there are no limits to the constitutionally guaranteed freedom of speech. In 1919 in Holms' ruling in Shenk vs. US proposed that there are limits to one's freedom of speech. His famous example was that no one has the right to shout fire in a theater. When a speech creates a clear and present danger to a universal moral standard, such as advocating hatred of other groups, then the constitutional guarantee of freedom of speech should be rescinded. Hence, when any person advocates ideas that can lead to the violation of other's rights to life and freedom and when it clearly creates danger to others existence such ideas should not be tolerated. At such occasions we must indeed become intolerant.

Let me hasten to add the following caveat. I am not opposed to tolerance, nor do I seek to deny that love provides an important contribution to the development of a quality of life. As of this writing I've been married sixty years and I doubt whether I could have overcome the effects of the Holocaust were it not for the love I received from my wife and children. The Talmudic rabbis have instructed us about the importance of love and they held up the love between David and Jonathan as an example of such love. David and Jonathan's love was a purely intrinsic love. Their relationship was so spiritual that the soul of Jonathan was bound with the soul of David. Such friendship is indeed rewarding. But, again, love cannot be universal. No person can love every one he encounters. Perhaps, love could have served as an integrative force in very small villages of the past – relationships that is represented in a gemeinshaft or in small communal societies guided by the principle of agape. In such a society the tolerance and perhaps the love of strangers could be intrinsic to that culture. This, of course would be the opposite

Faith and Conflict

of the culture of Sodom and Gomorrah. Tolerance, however, as I have pointed out is not an effective force in a highly pluralistic society. We need to find other moral values which can replace tolerance and overcome egoism and self orientation so common in a modern highly differentiated society in which everyone is seeking his own happiness rather than the happiness of the collective?

I would like to suggest that modern society's well being must be founded on the principle of justice. Jefferson in his inaugural address proposed that without justice freedom itself would be destroyed. What is needed is "equal and exact justice to all men, of whatever state of persuasion, religious and political." (31 Bellah et.al.)

Central to the concept "justice" is the idea of equity. For instance, justice in economic terms would assure the existence of equitable reciprocity between buyer and seller. Such equity could be expressed in terms of equity of value that is, that the money one offers the seller of an object reflects the equity of effort expended by the seller who is the creator of the object. If the seller, however, is not the creator of the product than the price should reflect the sellers investment and the effort required to bring the object to the market.*** Justice in contractual relationships is also based of an equitable exchange. To Durkheim(1984 chapter VII) any contract that reflects an inequitable relationship, even though agreed by both parties, is not valid. Justice demand that equity must exist in all human relationships. From this sense, just social relationship exists when all people in the system are given the same privileges and duties. The Bible tells us that in a just society the rich should not be honored in court for their wealth or power nor the poor to be favored because of his poverty.

Of course, human rights, in spite of Jefferson's reference that the Creator has endowed these on all human beings, are not divinely ordained but are social creations. Jefferson's reference to God is merely one of the means by which he seeks to legitimate the idea of equal access to rights. After all, throughout history, the name of God has also been used to deny both rights and love. Looking at the history of religion, particularly the history of Christianity, Feuerbach(1957) rightfully argues that "whenever morality is based on theology, whenever the right is made dependent on divine authority, the most immoral, unjust, infamous things can be justified and established. (Feuerbach 1957p.274.) My own experiences lead me to agree with Feuerbach. The history of Europe clearly points out that the Christian world has from its incipiency, in the name of God, denied Jews their right to an economic life and often to life itself. How well I remember that in 1938 the Hungarian government decreed by fiat that Jewish stores in my home town Munkacs should not exceed seven percent of the total. We have used many ways to legitimate human inequality. How many people accepted that the denial of life to Jews or that slavery has been ordained by God? The legitimacy of equitable human rights resides neither in God nor in any other supernatural force. Its legitimacy resides only in our accord that equitable justice is not only necessary to eliminate discord in a highly diversified society but that it is in its own right a moral imperative.

In the last two hundred years from the time that we crafted our constitution we have placed an inordinate stress on individual rights in society This is quite understandable. After all, our struggle for national independence was simultaneously a struggle for the individual's independence from an autocratic government. No wonder therefore that we have never placed equal emphasis on the other side of the coin, namely on individual's duties to the collective. Rights and corresponding duties, privileges and responsibilities are two sides of the same coin – they constitute the totality of justice. One cannot demand rights without also accepting his duties. In short, when we seek that governments grant us our individual rights we must also be willing to take on our duties to the government that represents the collective will. We have in many ways rejected our duties to the collective. We wish to be protected but at the same time we do not wish to serve in the armed forces.

Faith and Conflict

We wish to receive help when we encounter economic difficulties but quite often we are not willing to provide the necessary taxes that such help demands. There is a rising swell in public opinion that we have gone far a field in granting personal rights without requiring a commitment to corresponding duties and self help. This is most evident in opposition to the four decades of racial quota systems. In contrast to love and tolerance, rights and duties do not require that individuals must emphasize the ideals of care and love for others. I do not wish to deny that were we to develop personal virtues to teach people to become virtuous that it would perhaps also enhance the quality of life. After all, we develop a "nice" feeling when someone cares for us and is empathetic to our pain. But, even when people would develop personal virtues it will not alter the nature of social relationships. But when I am granted my rights and I accept my duties then I do not have to depend on the charity of being tolerated. Once I posses my rights and I am willing to accept also my duties then I can be free from discrimination. Under such conditions I need not come to the majority, hat in hand, and ask the powerful to tolerate me. When we achieve this type of society governed by justice we would have gone in the right direction toward the creation of an equitable and a more harmonious society.

Summary:

All societies' perception of human relationship arises out of two world views: empathy and concern for equity. Each of these views is rooted in the nature of the character of society. Toennies, the German sociologist of the late 1890's proposed that there are two types of societies which he named Gemeinschaft and Gesselschaft. The former is primarily agricultural and these usually small communities are religiously and ethnically homogeneous. In such societies the social relationship was reflected in the Western Christian world in an emphasis on kinship relationship, and mirrored the ideal of Agape. On the other hand, in a Gesselshaft a society that is composed of religious, occupational and ethnic heterogeneity social and economic relationships are fundamentally contractual relationships. Durkheim similarly proposes the existence of two types of societies. The earlier societies that were primarily occupationally homogeneous develop a form of unity that he calls mechanical solidarity. This unity is rooted in their homogeneity. In contrast the more diverse societies are united by an organismic force that is based on occupational interdependence and in such societies relationships are based on interchangeable needs which are governed by contractual relationship. Modern societies, both European and the United States are the latter type and hence such values as love and tolerance are no longer sufficient as an integrative force. Modern relationships if we seek to create a well functioning and relatively peaceful society are to be based primarily on justice namely a clear definition of rights and duties. Again, I do not wish to eliminate the importance of tolerance, we must understand, however, that it is only useful in individual personal relationships and not as a tool for achieving a harmonious modern social system.

Notes:

* This story was related to me by David Myerson's mother whose son is a friend of Derschowitz. 141
** Most studies on identity formation agree with George Herman Mead's view of the singular impact society has on its people.

Faith and Conflict

*** It is not our intention here to deal with the principle of equity in economics. I am using this merely as an example of the principle of justice.

References

1. Bendix, Reinhard 1956 Work and Authority in Industry
2. Berkley CA. University of California Press.
3. Durkheim, Emile 1984 The Division of Labor in Society trans. W.D. Halls New York The Free Press.
4. Feurbach, Ludwig.(1957) The Essence of Christianity New York Harper Torch Book
5. Fromm, Erich P. 1994 Escape from Freedom Owl Book edition.
6. Durkheim, Emile (1951) Suicide trans.Spaulding John A. and George Simpson. New York The Free Press.
7. Mannheim, Karl. 1955 Ideology and Utopia Harvest Books
8. Marx, Gary T. 1967 "Religion: Opiate or Inspiration of Civil Right Militancy Among Negroes" in American Sociological Review Vol.32 pp64-72
9. MacIntyre, Alasdair (1984) After Virtue University of Notre Dame Press
10. Mauss, Marcel Anne Sociologuique 1923-1924
11. Mead, G.H. 1934, Mind, Self, and Society Ed. C.W. Morris University of Chicago Press
12. Weber, Max 1958 The Protestant Ethic and the Spirit of Capitalism Charles Scribner's Sons. 142

Faith and Morals
Toward a Universal Moral
Infrastructure

The Holocaust was but one of the many tragedies Jews experienced in the last two millennia. It is also my personal tragedy. Like so many European Jews, I too have suffered the cruelties imposed on Jews by Nazi Germany. Like most European Jews I too have lost most members of my family, I have experienced harsh labor, starvation, and numerous beatings. I suppose that the injustices I experienced were one of the reasons why I chose sociology as my life's work. The questions to which I sought answers were why have the Jews been singled out in last two millennia to suffer by the hands of Christians, a religion advocates love? Could have the Holocaust been prevented? And finally, and most importantly, what are the issues and problems that need redress so that the Holocaust should not be repeated.

Anti-Jewish feelings and legalized atrocities against Jews began with the anti-Jewish edicts instituted by Constantine emperor of Rome in 350 C.E. This is not to say that Jews have not experienced tragedies before Constantine. Jews have fought and lost many wars. They lost their Temples twice. Judea and Israel has been occupied many times and its people were taken captive and as a consequence many have assimilated during their captivity and were eternally lost as Jewish

Faith and Conflict

world. These wars and associated tragedies before Constantine were not acts of anti-Semitism. They were political events similar to those that other nations have had to face since Cain slew Abel. For instance, Rome's wars against Israel and the destruction of the Temple, their subjugation and enslavement by Emperor Hadrian and Titus were politically motivated. However, Constantine's aggression toward Jews his anti-Jewish laws were non political unlike the earlier wars of destruction waged by Assyria and Persia. Constantine's anti Jewish laws were motivated purely by religion. Constantine's anti-Jewish edicts served as a model for most of the Christian countries for centuries to come. From Constantine's rule and on Jews in various countries and at various times were expelled from their domiciles and confined to specified locations now known as ghettos and very often they were killed by rabbles who were incited in various forms by the leaders of the Christian faiths. Only a cursory examination of European history will convince any reader to conclude that modern anti-Semitism had its roots in historic Christianity. Recently two published historical treatises <u>Papal Sin</u> and <u>Constantine's Sword</u> trace European anti-Semitism directly to the policies promulgated by the Catholic Church. Both authors accuse the church for the creation of a perspective, a religious milieu that ultimately led to Auschwitz and the Holocaust.

The Catholic Church under the leadership of John Paul has indirectly confessed to the church's historic sins against Jews and gave, what I can best describe, a very weak apology a poor expression of <u>mia culpa.</u> The apology issued by the Vatican in a document titled "We Remember" is indeed, as so many have noted, a perfunctory apology. "We Remember" was released in a press conference on March 16, 1998 over a half a century after Jews were liberated from the German Camps and five Popes after Pius the XII who ruled Vatican during the Holocaust and who was accused to have been a friend of Hitler. It is only after that many years that Pope John Paul presents this document and hopes that this declaration "will help to heal the wounds of past misunderstanding and injustices." Alas a true confession must follow with rectification of the causes that made the confession and the apology necessary in the first place. To this day such rectification has not been made.

I assume that the many Holocaust study programs that were introduced in Catholic universities and high schools in the United States were attempts to serve as rectification for past sins. However, neither the Catholic Church nor any other Christian denomination has eliminated or altered those perspectives and statements in the Christian Bible that many scholars believe contributed to the two millennia of anti-Semitism in the Western World. For instance in the Christian Bible John denounces the Jews stating "Ye are of your father the devil, and the lusts of your father ye will do. He was murdered from the beginning. (John 8:44) Matthew similarly denounces the Jews thusly. "But woe unto you, scribes and Pharisees, hypocrites ... Ye fools and blind ... Ye serpents, ye generation of vipers, how can ye escape the damnation of hell." (Matthew 23) Particularly the Forth Gospel is heavily anti-Jewish. In it Jews are referred to as the children of the Devil as John's Gospel does (John 8:44). Such teachings have had inflammatory affect against Jews." My grandmother has always cautioned me to avoid being on the streets of her village during Easter when the priests each year gave the same sermon accusing Jews of deicide. Feuerbach (1957) describes the impact the New Testament had on Jews very succinctly. "The believer" writes Feuerbach "is blessed, well-pleasing to God, a partaker of felicity; the unbeliever is accursed, rejected of God and abjured by men: for what God rejects man must not receive, must not indulge; –that would be a criticism of the divine judgment" (253) This view is still a dominant among Catholics and has been reiterated in 1999 in the Vatican document Dominus Jesus written by then cardinal Retzinger (presently Pope Benedict). The Biblical description of Pilate's trial of Jesus tells us that when the Jews selected to Barabbas instead of Jesus for being pardoned the Jews damned themselves by proclaiming

Faith and Conflict

that the blood of Christ shall be upon the heads of all future generation of Jews. These anti Jewish perspectives are not merely a part of Catholic theology but it also became part of the theology of the Reformation and is evident in Luther's book "On the Jews and their Lies. Luther calls the Jews "poisonous envenomed worms." Like the Spanish inquisitors who expelled the Jews from Spain and Portugal, Luther too sought to have the Jews expelled from Saxony in 1537. His followers sacked the Berlin synagogue in 1572 and then the Jews were banned from the entire country. There are those like Michael Berenbaum who "In The World Must Know', the official publication of the United States Holocaust Museum, writes that Luther's reliance on the Bible as the sole source of Christian authority fed his fury against Jews over their rejection of Jesus as the messiah. When the Jews in Germany failed to convert, Luther turned on them. Berenbaum quotes Luther who declared "We are at fault in not slaying them. Rather we allow them to live freely in our midst despite their murder, cursing, blaspheming, lying and defaming." I wonder the extent to which Luther's view of the Jews influenced Karl Marx's views expressed in his book On the Jewish Question. Of course, I must assume that Luther's views must have had an influence of the German people's acceptance of the Nazi views of Jews and their desire to accomplish the Final Solution.

I recently attended a conference in which a Catholic high school teacher in Atlanta spoke about the church's historical contribution to anti-Semitism. While such admission is gratifying he could not provide any solution to the problem. When I asked what solutions would he recommend so that the church would eliminate historic anti-Semitism the speaker became bewildered and could not suggest any other idea than the oft abused concept: tolerance. The best he could suggest was that Christian churches must teach their adherents greater awareness of other cultures and religions and thereby develop a tolerance to diversity. Not only is the teaching of tolerance is both too little and too late but as I have argued elsewhere tolerance as a value hardly solves the problem of intolerance (Is Tolerance Adequate in this book). In fact tolerance,

I proposed, justifies and reinforces the conditions that made tolerance necessary in the first place. The source for Christian hostility of Jews is deeply rooted in the Christian Bible. "If the Church is indeed concerned with the elimination of its anti-Jewish attitude" I commented to the teacher "should it not begin by eliminating the Biblical teaching that led to anti-Semitism?" The teacher was unable to respond to my comment. After all, changing the tone of the Bible either by eliminating its intolerant teaching or at least trying to re-interpret them is something that must be started by the one whose teaching and dicta is considered to be infallible – the Pope himself and this is most unlikely to occur. Similarly, after devoting hundreds of pages in which Carroll cogently argues that Catholic teachings were central to European anti-Semitism he is unable to provide equally cogent propositions what the church could do to eliminate the continued anti- Semitic perspective in Christianity.

Thomas Jefferson, whom I consider to have had the keenest mind among the founding fathers, commented that he considered the Christian Bible to be the source of hostilities against other religions, he suggested that all newly elected representatives be given a razor and the New Testament and they should proceed to eradicate all those teachings that have been detrimental to social life. * Anti-Jewish sentiment and associated hostile action against them was not limited to the Christian world alone. The Muslim world, too, has from the eighth century on, following the teaching of Quran particularly those in the fifth Surah, made life for Jews within Muslim world difficult. In a sense, present Arab hostilities against Israel are not of recent origin. It is not a reaction merely to the rise of the State of Israel. It is the continuation of an anti-Jewish attitude associated with the rise Islam. This point of view expressed by Mohamed in spite the help given to him by the Jews of Medina who hid him to protect him from the wrath of his own

Faith and Conflict

people. Jews were an essential part of the Hijra in 620 C.E. It should be interesting to note that there existed a period that in the Jewish history called "the golden age" a two hundred year period (778 -1013) in Spain when Muslim tolerance of Jews has indeed led to two centuries of great cultural productivity. This, however, was an aberration in the history of Jewish and Islamic relationships which for the most part was anti-Jewish.

In spite that the adherents of the three faiths who identify themselves as being the Children of Abraham they do not follow the spirit of their father Abraham. Abraham was a non proselytizing seeker of peace who confronted God and pleaded the cause of Sodom and Gomorrah. Instead of being seekers of peace like Abraham, Christian and Muslim behavior toward each other reflects a sibling rivalry and jealousy. Each religion in the historical order of their appearance, argued that they, and they alone acquired the newest and freshest information regarding God's wishes particularly what pleases God and what He wants from us. Each religion in its succession claimed that they alone have merited being the recipient of God's newest revelation and the newest religions have always proposed that the older revelations which incidentally were the foundation on which they declared their own legitimacy, although interesting, do not represent the latest in the prophetic truths. The new religions also argue that the older religion's truth claims are false. It is the faithful who contend that they alone are privileged of having a special relationship with God that that in their mind eye legitimates their sense of superiority over others. This blindness to the truths in other religions must lead me to state that faith is the root of arrogance.

The rejection of the older prophetic views and associated theologies together with the new religions belief that only they hold the true and valid path to God creates an interesting paradox. If on the one hand all three religions espouse the belief that God is eternal, and all knowing, and hence He is a-historical, how then is it possible that God with time also changes his mind? If God is not subject to human limitations such as time related discovery of knowledge why then didn't He reveal the whole truth the first time when he spoke to mankind? And if He did, then where is the logic in later revelations? The validity of all revelations must hence rest on the assumption that they reflect a human's view of God and not God's revelation of himself. It is illogical to hold the belief that if God is not subject to human need of time based discovery why then does God need to change His point of view and give new revelations? Doesn't such a view defy the principle of God's eternality?

The Talmudic rabbis argued for instance, that since the Torah was given by God it is not subject to historical chronology, as they expressed it "there is no earliness or lateness in the Torah." After if all the future and the past is to God an eternal present then the first revelation should be considered immutable. How then can we logically justify the validity of piecemeal revelations? On the other hand Christianity and Islam by accepting the validity of later revelations denies God eternity because God's is himself subject later discoveries and hence his knowledge like our knowledge is evolutionary.

Newer religions, however, cannot reject the idea of God's infallibility otherwise the new religions cannot claim that the later revelations given to them and them alone are valid. Most likely this illogical argumentation will continue to exist and new revelations will claim their validity in the same manner because belief is not based on logic but on non-logical faith. In the future I am sure new religions will arise (other than the Church of the Latter Day Saints) that will seek to negate the legitimacy of the three earlier views of God and with it add new causes to religious wars and associated hatreds.

The problem is that those who claim to possess God's new revelations and the owners of the old claims rigidify their positions and stand in a form of a dialectical opposition to each other. Perhaps the most potentially inflammable religious view that has led to inter-religious hostility is the view of blasphemy. Central to the definition of blasphemy is that the adherents of one religion see the other beliefs as being

Faith and Conflict

contemptuous and irreverent of their God. It is this perception that has been and continues to be the core cause to inter-religious violence. Each religion, through the use of violence seeks to protect the validity and honor of their God.

Why does the perception of others religious beliefs seeming irreverence of the new churches view of God lead to anger? Perhaps because the faithful believe that God needs protection and that the faithful must avenge God's honor otherwise God will not bestow his goodness and grace to the faithful. In a sense we treat God in similar manner as we treat our country. We get equally angry if someone in our view is irreverent to our nation. We become disturbed when another nation dishonors our flag and we wish to take revenge otherwise our nation loses its power and prestige. People's attitude to God and to their nation is very similar. (The interrelationship between God and the nation is well argued by Emile Durkheim in The Elementary forms of Religious Life.) However, if we get angry and seek revenge on people who deny our vision of God and His existence and thereby seek to protect God aren't we therefore also denying God's power? Do we have to become God's big brother and feel that we must defend His honor? Aren't we hence diminishing God's stature and His independence of mortals or His sense of justice if we believe that He will punish the faithful believers if they do not stand up and defend His honor and dignity? It is undeniable that every time someone seeks to defend God's honor and His revealed truth and the validity of His existence he ends up reducing God not only to human level but to a weak human being who depends on big brother to defend his dignity. This is exactly what Moses did when he tried to influence go and declared to him "What will the Egyptians say?"

Moses juxtaposes God with the Egyptian Gods and tell Him that if he destroys the Israelites it will make him appear weak and powerless. Defending God reduces God's power and transcendence instead of accepting Him as the powerful and independent transcendental entity

He really is. The truth of the matter is that what we are really protecting is not God but the power, the status, and prestige of those who claim to speak for God.

Religion and the state have always been united and God is used as the symbolic representation of the nation. In short we state: When you defile my God you defile my nation. Although we argue that we have long overcome the idea of a national God or a national religion the truth of the matter is that we have not done so and because of it we continue to suffer the associated intolerances.

One of the first persons to perceive the problems associated with the rigidity of religion and how adherence to one belief leads to hostilities with other faiths was Ludwig Feuerbach. In 1850 he published his controversial tome The Essence of Christianity in which he takes a critical view on religion in general and on Christianity in particular. In it he rightly perceives that one common feature of all faiths is that faith with time turns into dogma and leads to hate and persecution of the adherents of other faiths. Faith, proposes Feuerbach, is blind to the existence of goodness and truth in other religions. In short, Feuerbach proposes, something that we all know – religion is highly particularistic. Very often Christians have expressed their great sorrow for me because as a Jew I will never achieve salvation and will be eternally damned. Of course the corollary to this is: If God damns me why should not the Christians do the same? I have quite often seen Christian love in action namely, that Christians out of their love and concern for me wish to convert me and thus avert the surety of my damnation. It is clear that such a view is and cannot be tolerant of other religions. Religious wars are wars of faiths and peace cannot be established so long as faith is taken as dogma.

A century before Feuerbach's critical analysis of religion Gotthold Ephraim Lessing, author and critic, was distressed by the hatred and intolerance that exists between the three major religions. Lessing was pained by the hostilities that German Christians afflicted Jews. He was

Faith and Conflict

deeply saddened that because of the Christian beliefs his friend a rabbi, philosopher, and scholar Moses Mendelssohn had to endure mistreatments. Lessing was seeking a paradigm by which different religions could develop an ideology of peace and co-existence. He presented his ideas of religious unity in his most famous play <u>Nathan the Wise</u>. In his story the protagonist Nathan was modeled after his friend Moses Mendelssohn.

Briefly, Nathan, a Jew and an employee of a Sultan was asked by his employer, a Muslim, which of the three religions, Judaism, Islam, and Christianity is the true religion. Nathan found himself on the horns of a dilemma. He could not propose that Judaism, his own religion, is the one and only true religion because by so doing he will denounce Islam which may lead to his demise. Of course, he cannot proclaim the supremacy of Islam because by this act he will deny his own faith and at the same time he will also eliminate any reason why he should not chose to become a Muslim. Should he Nathan proclaim that Lessing's religion Christianity to be the true religion he then would violate the Sultan's and his own faith.

To solve this problem and argue for the equality of all religion Nathan relates the parable of the rings. The story tells of a father who possess a magical ring that brings good fortune to its possessor. The ring was a family treasure and each father before he died gave the ring and the instruction how to activate its magic to his most beloved son. This father now had three sons whom he loved equally. As he became old the father was seeking a solution to his problem. How could he leave his heritage the magical ring to each of his sons? He called in a gold smith and asked him to make two exact duplicates of the original ring and upon completion to bring all three rings to him so that he himself would not know which is the original and true ring. The gold smith did as he was requested. Now as the father lay dying he asked each son, to visit him alone. During the visit each son was given the supposedly true magical ring and the instructions how to make the ring work. Each son was told that to invoke the magical potential of the ring so that it brings him good fortune, the wearer must certain requirements: He must be kind, truthful, and honest. The father speaking to each son alone hands him the ring and tells him that he should not divulge the receipt of the ring to the others. The father dies and at the funeral the brothers see that each of them is wearing the ring that they thought they were its sole possessor. Each, hence, became jealous of the other and each now argued that he alone is the possessor of the true ring and the others have fakes ones.

To keep peace in the family they decide to separate themselves geographically. However, since each of them firmly believed the he is the owner of the true ring he tried to activate the ring's magic by the appropriate attitude and belief and behold all of them became successful.

Although Lessing sought to claim the efficacy of all religions as long as their adherents follow its teachings he fails to do so. Just because the sons did not know who has the true ring, the old ring, the heritage ring, the story does not negate its existence as the true ring. All that the father has accomplished was to create a hostile atmosphere in which jealousy and mistrust.

Inter religious hostility still rules. Although Vatican II tried to create religious ecumenism, however, it was limited the various factions of Christianity. Other religions were excluded. The problem of religious intolerance and inter religious hostilities continues to exist because the different religions cannot and will not create a common infrastructure that on the one hand will unite all adherers to various beliefs while at the same time still leave room for differences in their faiths that are founded on different experiences.

The problem is that each religion advocates that it alone reflects the true faith. The present Pope, in attempt to create unity between Christians and Jews declared that only Christianity and Judaism are true faiths and no other religion can legitimately claim of being a faith. He thus excludes the millions of Muslims and even more billions of others.

Faith and Conflict

We have seen and experienced in the last eight decades that what Feuerbach has cautioned us about faith, namely that with time it "passes into hatred, [and] hatred into persecution." This causal relationship does exist. Moreover as Feuerbach proposed, because faith is solely concerned with man's duty and obligations to God faith cares little or not at all with man's relationship with man. The love of God, if anything, deprives us from loving man. There will be those who will argue: that the essence of Christian faith is the belief in the supremacy of love. After all, one can refer to the Christian Bible that proposes the He who knows not love doesn't know God – for God is love. But Feuerbach again caution's us that what the Bible really teaches is "To love the man who does not believe in Christ, is a sin against Christ, it is to love the enemy of Christ." (253) Moreover he continues "He who loves the men whom Christ denies, [who do] not believe in Christ, denies his Lord and God. Faith abolishes the natural ties of humanity; to universal, natural unity, it substitutes a particular unity." (254)

Faith in every sense is opposite to morality which is the foundation on which men's relationship with men is founded. "It is morality alone" proposes Feuerbach "and by no means faith, that cries out in the conscience of the believer: thy faith is nothing, if it does not make thee good." (262) With an absence of moral commitment faith becomes the reason for war – for it is faith that demands that we guard God's honor – for God is a jealous God who demands that we sacrifice ourselves for his name. This and this alone had developed in the three faiths the worship of martyrs. In short, the more we give to God the less we have left to be concerned with mankind.

Why then do we commit ourselves to the primacy of faith? This was indeed the central question asked by Jean Paul Sartre in his play the Flies. Like Erich From, Sartre also proposes that faith relieves us from torments is associated with difficulties experienced in living. Faith assures us that so long as we commit ourselves to the deity we need not have fear of the future even unto death. Faith is the bosom of God's comfort. And in spite of the particularistic nature of faith, people still seek to find a way for developing a belief in human universalism. Of course most religions advocated a unity – but they advocate a unity that is based on an adherence to a common faith —theirs. The Catholic Church, for instance sees itself as the Universal Church and argues that it can provide a unity if all people would adhere to the Church's teachings.

Similar views are held by Islam. The Jewish belief system makes it possible to have different faith and still achieve salvation.

This is similar to Simmel's argument that war can be beneficial in so far that by destroying opposition one in the end creates a unity. In a similar manner if we eliminate all other faiths, of course, we would ipso facto eliminate religious conflict. Religions have tried and failed to proselytize and hoping to convert all people to their faith. They also failed in using power, as early Christians and as Muslims. The Crusades and the wars of Islamic that were influenced by the belief in Sword of Allah are essentially very similar. Religions, as hard as they tried, could not bring about the destruction of other faiths. For the sake of mankind they must learn to co-exist with other faiths. Unity can exist even among diverse faiths. It can exist only when religions place primacy on a common moral perspective and not on faith. Faiths can and must remain independent from moral teaching. Faith should remain as a set of beliefs that on the one hand ties the individual to a transcendent. It should remain in the domain of the spirit, the belief in surety of the future. But, on the other hand, morals, unlike faith, are based on the principle of "common humanism" something that people of different faiths and non believers alike can share. In short, to advance humanism all religions should not advocate a faith that separates us from others but a faith which advocates the unity that we share with the transcendent. But, at the same time, faiths must become secondary to the teaching of man's relationship with man, namely a common moral system.

Faith and Conflict

The Unitarian Church to their credit attempted to create a religion that would teach the validity of all faith. This was also its weakness. A Talmudic saying states "he who claims to have encompassed everything encompasses nothing." Just as political perspectives differ among people because people have different life experiences so do faiths. The Jews' historical experiences differ from other European and Asiatic people and hence their view of God, of the transcendent, and the nature of salvation will also differ. People can intellectually understand other faiths and beliefs but do not share the emotional sense and the commitment that the faithful have to their beliefs. I can, for instance enjoy liturgical music of other faith, but my enjoyment of it is purely based on my appreciation of its music. It does not elicit in me the same sense of awe as for instance as the music of the Kol Nidre the ancient music with which the Day of Atonement services start. Some time ago I looked at the Unitarian hymnal that catered to people with varied religious experiences. For instance, next to the Christmas carols were Hanukah songs. This admixture of songs reminded me of the Captain of the floundering ship in which Jonah sought to flee from performing his duty. The ship was in imminent danger of sinking. In the face of this danger the captain asked all the people on the ship to pray each to his god perchance one of them will listen. Religion can not be a cocktail in which we take a measure of each beliefs shake and serve. Christmas and Chanukah are symbols of two different historical events. During the Christmas season and because of the television I sometimes hum Christmas songs. I however, unlike Christians do not have an emotional attachment to these songs as I do for Chanukah songs.

Faith is both a single person's and the collective's mode of relationship and interaction with the transcendent. Although people share a particular faith none the less individuals within the faith develop a unique view of God, one that he or she does not share with the collective. It is the product one's personal experiences and hence it differs among individuals. It is the trust that a person has in a transcendent and in spite of lack of evidence he none the less maintains his faith and trust in his god and his power. It is a person's view of a particular God that provides an essential human need namely the negation of nihilism. Unlike empirical view of life religion allays the fear that life is nothing else but that what we experience and that death is the final stage of existence. Of course not all people need the same degree of reassurance that life is meaningful and that death is not the end of existence. At the same time each individual also shares a collective experience that includes a common human experience arising out of man's relationship with nature and each other – in short we share elements of a common life experience. These life experiences of making a living of having to relate with others sharing a common attitude toward needs like medicine and justice provides the common denominator to a universal moral system. It is the moral norms arising out of shared experiences of living that should become the infra-structure on which collective relationship should be based and religion needs to support this form of morality. This is evidenced in the prophetic teaching in the Jewish Bible. Religion must not only provide hope for life after death but more importantly it must provide hope for existence in this life. No society can exist without a moral teaching of justice that specifies both our rights, that is our legitimate expectations <u>vis a vis</u> other individuals and society as a whole and even more importantly our duties to others and to society.

The problem today is that people espouse a faith based morality which like faith becomes a source of divisiveness. Faith based morality if often justified simply by the belief that it is God who defines what is moral or immoral.

In Judaism religious laws consist of "Hukim" or a Mishpatim. Hukim are those laws that one must accept without relying on logic and reasoning. These are ritual laws that are ordained by God and one accepts them on faith alone. Some time ago my wife related to me that when her Christian friends asked her why Jews keep kosher she

Faith and Conflict

proposed, as so many do, that it is a cultural remnant of early Jews approach to health issues. Of course some elements of Kashruth (keeping kosher) can be seen as being health related for instance the injunction against eating meats that are more than three days old or the eating of found animal carrion. Meats that stand for three days without refrigeration should have been suspect as a health hazard to all especially those who live in warm climates. But at the same time this theory cannot rationally explain why one is permitted to eat locusts, grasshoppers and crickets but cannot eat lobsters. Hukim are hence God ordained laws that, according the Orthodox Jewish point of view, one must accept and follow without question. They are commandments. Similarly homosexuality is perceived as immoral not because such behavior is detrimental to the well being of the collective but because to the faithful it is one of the hukim. God defined homosexuality as immoral and God's decrees cannot be challenged. Proscription that cannot be understood as having reference to constituted moral order even though it is claimed to be God ordained. Morals, if they are to be accepted as valid, must be understood from a rational point of view. Thus morals are those pro and prescriptions that are necessary to maintain the well being of both individuals and the collective. Faith and morals constitute separate human domains and therefore faith and morals should not be interrelated. Faith based ordinances that are sometimes fallaciously believed to be morals. They are not. They are the non logical acceptance of God ordained ordinances and therefore carry with them all the flaws inherent in faith itself.

The more we become technologically advanced the more we become dependent on each other to provide us with the necessities of life. Three centuries ago the idea of individual freedom rested in land ownership. If one owned land he had the means with which to be independent from others because most people shared a common knowledge.

In modern societies however, the need for interdependence is more acute and its achievement is more complex. No individual can remain alive solely based on his own knowledge and skills alone. Durkheim (1984) in his discourse On the Division of Labor in Society shows that social life today consists of an intricate web of interdependence founded on our needs of specialized labor that is performed by other persons. Today, no individual alone possesses all the knowledge and skills necessary for his continued existence. The key phrase that characterizes today's economy is division of labor. I could not exist today, especially in my old age with its infirmities, if I would not have access to an internist, cardiologist, rheumatologist, and urologist just as I could not survive without a butcher, baker etc.

While economic diversity creates a need for greater interdependence This requirement, however, is made more difficult by the ever increasing religious diversity and inter- faith hostilities. The problem of hostilities that arise from religious diversity was one of the central concerns to the Prophet Isaiah. The first one to see the needs for universal unity was espoused by Malachi who raises the following questions: Have we not all one father? Hath not God created us? Why do we deal treacherously every man against his brother, by profaning the covenant of our father? (Chp.10) Micah reduced moral requirements to three ideals. He tells us that God merely wants three things, to do justice, to love mercy, and to walk humbly before the Lord. Following in this path the Talmudic rabbis sought a common denominator that will serve as a uniting force in human relationship.

To accomplish this task they redefined how salvation, one of the major human concerns, can be acquired. Christianity proposes that salvation is achieved through faith alone. Hence, those who do not accept the tenets of their faith cannot achieve everlasting life and will be subject to the harsh punishment reserved to the unbelievers. The rabbis proposed that instead of faith the road that leads to salvation is through morality. Behavior and not faith, they proposed, leads to eternal life. It is what you do to others and not what you believe that counts. One can

Faith and Conflict

point to the Biblical stories and see that God never sought to punish the world for the absence of faith but for the absence of moral behavior.

Cain was marked because he murdered his brother. The flood was brought on because "the Lord saw how great was man's wickedness on earth, and how every plan devised by his mind was nothing but evil all the time." (Genesis 6:5) Similarly the destruction of Sodom and Gomorrah was precipitated because of their wickedness. The practice of evil and injustice was the root core for God's intent to destroy Nineveh the capital of Assyria.

I have been taught that after death the soul comes before God's holy throne where He sits in judgment. In front of Him there is a scale where on one end of the scale the person's good deeds are placed and on the other end his evil deeds. If his good deeds exceed the evil deeds, then he is rewarded with life in Paradise but, if his evil and immoral deeds exceed his good deeds he is judged to be punished. Jews believe that God's judgment is universal. He judges all people on the same scale. People are judged on their performance of justice and not based on love. The question that is central in the heavenly court is: has the person standing in judgment treated others with justice? Faith in the existence of God or his surrogate is not an essential element for achieving salvation.

The Talmudic rabbis hence proposed a common denominator, a set of moral teaching without which humanity cannot exist because without adhering to it the world becomes evil. This common moral denominator is the Noahite Laws. I prefer to think of these principles as God's universal covenant with Adam. Underlying this set of moral laws is the belief that mankind is a unity. This view is expressed in the following rabbinic explanation associated with the creation of Adam. "Why" asked a rabbi "did God create mankind by creating Adam a single and solitary person? This is quite unlike the creation of all other animals when He simultaneously created many of the same species." The reason answered the rabbi is that "no one should later say I am more important than you because of my ancestors were more important." Following the same reasoning no one can say I am better than you because I follow a different belief. It is not belief – but deeds that count and the good and moral deeds are those that improve human life. The Talmud teaches us that he who saved one life is like he saved the whole world. The rabbis do not say he who saves a Jewish life because from their point of view all life is equally sacred.

What then constitutes the rabbinic the common denominator of the universal morality? These are:

1. You shall practice equity, establish and promote justice.
2. You shall not commit Idolatry
3. You shall not commit Blasphemy
4. You shall not commit Sexual Immorality
5. You shall not commit Murder
6. You shall not commit Theft
7. You shall not eat the limb torn from a live animal. Flesh with the life in it, the blood of it, you shall not eat.

These principles were elaborated two millennia ago. Of course they do not necessarily reflect present day thoughts. However, the significance of these principles is that it provides a model on which present day a common set of morality sans faith can be established which then becomes the basis by which the human world can be unified. Of course not all of these principles especially the prescriptions against idolatry and blasphemy are necessarily valid today. What is important is that the rabbis were seeking moral principles that can exist and be a part of all people regardless of their religious faiths. Adhering to these principles does not deny one's the right to have diverse ways to seek a relationship with the transcendent. Two thousand years ago it was inconceivable that a functioning moral system can exist without being attached to the fear of a punishing God. However, today, there are a

Faith and Conflict

substantial number of people who will accept the proposition of morality as the guiding principle of human life without subscribing to any religious belief.

No one can dispute the idea that life in a society cannot exist without the principle of equity and justice. To me, as I have proposed in other essays, justice is based on the ideal that all human beings have equal right to access the necessities for the maintenance of life. More importantly, to paraphrase an ancient Jewish principle: All people are responsible for each other. However, the principle of justice cannot be based solely on one person's responsibility to others without completing the human equation namely that my responsibilities are only the one side of the human equation. The other side are my duties to society and the people in it. In short human relationships must be based on equitable reciprocal relationships. My duties to others must be completed by the other person's duties toward me. If I grant others rights, reciprocally, others must grant me equal rights. Thus, if I must help other to have the means of life at the same time it is the responsibility of the others to labor for the needs that others depend on their life. As I proposed, believing in a God is neither necessary nor required for a moral order to exist. Reciprocal human relationships can be guided by the power of the collective will based on reason. Durkheim has already shown that the power that we endow on God is merely the sanctification of the power of the collective. However, in his study of suicide Durkheim has also pointed out that the emotional well being of people are directly related to the belief and acceptance of the existence of a transcendental entity. No person can be emotionally complete without accepting that there is something greater than the individual himself. This belief is not mandatory. It is merely a suggestion that there is a greater force, or even a principle that is greater than the individual himself can enhance one's life. Still, this belief is necessary for the well being of the collective. We all need to have a meaning for life and that meaning is fundamentally tied to membership in a collective. The great success of the television program Roots attests to a people's desire for belonging and being attached to a transcendental entity.

It is not my intention here to re-interpret the Noahite Laws but merely to show as Kohlberg had done in his writing that certain moral precepts are universal. The moral views are the products of common human experiences as members of society. Perhaps the most significant of these are those moral precepts that are related to maintain social equilibrium. It is now necessary that those morals relating to social equilibrium be treated as universal morals. It is only when we seek to control not only inter- societal but also intra-societal aggressions that we can provide for a peaceful social co-existence. Religion can assume a leadership in the formation of universal morals. However, it can do so only if they renounce the limitations imposed by faith.

Notes:

* This was related by Christopher Hitchens, a Jefferson biographer in a televised segment in the Miami Book Festival. References

Reference:

1. Carroll, James 2001 Constentine Sword Mariner Books
2. Berenbaum, Michael The World Must Know New York: Shapolowsky
3. Durkheim, Emile 1984 The Division of Labor In Society trans W.D. Halls, The Free Press.

Faith and Conflict

4. Durkheim, Emile 1965 The Elementary Forms of the Religious Life New York The Free Press
5. Feuerbach, Ludwig 1957 The Essence of Cristianity trans. George Eliot Harper and Row
6. Kohlberg, Lawrence, 1981 "From Is to Ought" in Essays on Moral Development Vol.I San Francisco Harper and Row.
7. Lessing, Gotthold E. 2004 Nathan the Wise Boston St. Martin Press
8. Luther, Martin 2008 Nathan the Wise Kindle Edition
9. Sartre, Jean Paul 1976 "The Flies" in No Exist and three other plays.
10. N.Y. Vintage International 11.Wills, Garry 2000 Papal Sin: Structures of Deceit Double Day 163

Epilogue

Remember the Holocaust

Forgetting difficult and painful events and experiences is perhaps one the greatest gifts that God endowed on mankind. Without the capacity to forget it would be extremely difficult to live because the pains of the past would constantly would multiply and be felt. Without the capability to forget we couldn't recuperate from tragedies, and in the words of a popular song, pick ourselves up and start over again. Without forgetting the pain of childbirth, for instance, most women would be extremely reluctant to have more children. Without forgetting the pain of a spouse's death or the experience of a divorce, there probably wouldn't be remarriages. For a long time, for instance, I was unable to talk, write, and analyze my holocaust experiences — the pain of my experiences in the Holocaust, the loss of my family, starvation, beatings was too excruciating. I needed to forget. It is only by distancing myself from these experiences was I able to re-establish a semblance of normalcy to my life. I needed to forget so that my conscious thoughts wouldn't be governed by cynicism and hatred and my nights disturbed by nightmares.

Yet, there are events both personal and collective ones that should not be forgotten. For by confronting and understanding such events

Faith and Conflict

can we hope to eliminate from happening again. Very frequently when I lecture on my Holocaust experiences the audience, be they high school or college students and adults ask me: "Could such events happen again?" Sometimes they even ask me: "Could it happen in the United States?" Reluctantly I must disturb them with my answer: "yes it could." It is only if we examine truthfully and honestly the reasons why the Holocaust has happened and learn from it, only then can us possibly prevent another future holocaust.

All nations and religions have established days of remembrances. In the United States we are instructed to remember the Alamo. We instituted Veterans Day, Memorial Day, and Independence Day all which have been designed to remind us of certain American experiences. France has its Bastille Day and Hungary its independence day and so on.

From Biblical time on Jews were instructed to remember the tragedies that have befallen on them. The Bible instructs the Jews to remember Amalek and the immoral way they waged wars against them in the desert right after they departed from Egypt. The Bible repeatedly instructs the Jews to remember Egypt. Remember, it instructs the Jews, that you have been slaves in Egypt where you have been made to suffer. Each summer after I turned thirteen I had to fast on the ninth days of the Hebrew month of Av. The fasting and the reading of Jeremiah's lamentations were to remind us of the destruction of both Temples. Most nations have instituted days of remembrance. And yet why should we remember especially when remembering is associated with pain and forgetting contrarily would relieve us from the pain brought on by past problems? Remembering the Holocaust is, for instance, quite painful for me as it is for most of the survivors. And yet, I must not only remember but I must remind others about the event. Why? What do we gain from remembering?

The Bible instructs us to remember Amalekite and the Egyptian experience. The first is associated with need to take The Amalekites violated the moral rules of war. When the Jewish people left Egypt, the Amalekites attacked them from the rear where the women, the children and the infirm walked. Because of this immoral act, for their violation of the moral elements in warfare they should be destroyed. All of us who survived the camps can understand the desire to take sweet revenge. Taking vengeance, however, is not a Jewish value. The instruction of taking vengeance is contrary to all the moral teachings found in the Bible. It contradicts another Biblical command that cautions us that "vengeance is mine said the Lord." The Talmudic rabbis informed us that we the descendants of Abraham do not take vengeance instead we are seekers of peace. Taking revenge accomplishes nothing. By taking Revenge on moral offenders we not solve the problem of the evil that led some individuals or nations, in the first place, to commit the wrongs against others. Vengeance merely reinforces hatred and elicits a desire in the others for vengeance. In short vengeance creates a repetitive cycle in which A the wronged seeks to take vengeance on B who then considers himself as the wronged party which is to be solved by their vengeance on A. We must guard ourselves from wanting to take revenge because it never leads to peace. To the contrary, revenge merely creates, perpetuates and solidifies a circle of hatred and war. This type of remembering is exemplified by the tribal wars in Africa and the wars in former Yugoslavia. Memories that lead to a desire for revenge are called in Hebrew "zichronoth levataloh" that is useless and meaningless memories. Such memories do not elevate our humanity nor do they serve any moral ends.

But the taking of vengeance seems to be a universal response by parties that consider themselves to have been wronged. The injunction to take vengeance on the Amalekites is similar to the US injunction: Remember the Alamo. We are told to remember so that we should take revenge on those who in the present day represent Santa Anna.

Faith and Conflict

I remember seeing a statue in Mexico City that depicts Americans as a cruel conquering enemy whom the Mexicans are told not to trust. A similar statue also exists in Quebec, Canada. Each Passover in the Seder ceremony Jews hope for the coming of the of the prophet Elijah who will announce the coming of the redeemer, the messiah, who will avenge the many indignities, pain, and death the Jews have suffered in the last two millennia in the Christian world.

I must reject the idea that the purpose of remembering is to take revenge. Revenge solves nothing. It does not erase the past indignities. To the contrary, it merely enhances existing hostilities. Vengeance does not heal the pains of the past it merely tears of the scabs that began to bring healing. We must remember and recount the Holocaust even when these memories violate our Jewish moral dicta not to cause pain to any living thing, especially to ourselves. We must remember so that we should enter into a healing dialogue between the parties in the conflict for only understanding the issues in the conflict can lead to peaceful solutions

This idea is associated with the Biblical command to remember the experiences of slavery in Egypt. This command to remember the Jewish experiences in Egypt is not for purposes of taking revenge on them instead it is to serve as a teaching device for moral enhancement. Human progress, especially the progress of civilization, of morality, and, of humanism, as opposed to technological progress, comes only from a critical and conscious examination our deeds, be they individual or collective. Only when we own up to and confess our guilt can we advance our moral existence. Jewish concern with moral advancement that needs to be harvested from negative experiences is clearly demonstrated when Jews are instructed to remember their slavery in Egypt.

In spite of the four hundred years of torturous slavery, the hard work, and the killing of the first born sons, Jews are cautioned not to take vengeance on the Egyptians. To the contrary, the Torah instructs us to make the Egyptian experience the infrastructure for our morals and values. We are told that our experiences of slavery in Egypt, although tragic, should teach us not to follow the Egyptian morals but instead when they will establish their own country it should be based on the moral associated with justice. We are told to remember Egypt in order that we may learn from our slavery and suffering so that we may develop empathy for others and therefore not to inflict such terrible and inhumane acts on them. The Egyptian experience has laid the foundation for the Jewish moral view of "tzar baal chay", namely that it is our moral duty to refrain of committing painful acts on any living thing how much more so on human beings. The memory of Egyptian slavery has also become the foundation on which Jewish ideals of justice and democracy are based. Because of our experiences in Egypt, the Torah teaches us, there shall be but one law governing the rights of citizens, residents, and the strangers. Remembering Egypt is not a memory in vain. It is a memory for the enhancement of a moral order. The Torah uses the Egyptian experiences to develop in us a moral consciousness and sensitivity for the minorities, for the poor, the strangers, and the helpless in our society which is the basis of a constitutional democracy.

Each spring, Jewish communities worldwide observe Yom Hashoah – The Day of Remembrance – a day designated to remember those who perished in the Holocaust. Each year we Jews, at least some of us, force ourselves to remember, to remind ourselves and the world of the horrors European Jews suffered by hands of the Germans. Wouldn't it be far better all around for Jews and non Jews alike to forget the Holocaust rather than to relive the pain brought on by these memories? My answer is: Of course we must remember! For only by remembering such events will we also raise questions about the cause of evil that brought on not only the Holocaust but the two thousand years of anti-Semitism. This view led me to raise the questions which I try to answer in my essays.

Which of these two models of remembering should we apply to the Holocaust? Should the injunction to remember the Holocaust be similar to the one that instructs to remember Amalek – purely for the

Faith and Conflict

purpose of taking revenge? Or, should we treat the Holocaust as we treat the memory of Egypt namely an opportunity to further or moral development? I choose the latter.

One of the great commandments in the Torah is that we, the Jewish people should follow the precept to study and to teach. We should follow the ideals set in the Torah which have been exemplified by our prophets and Talmudic rabbis to learn from our experiences and teach and teach the enhanced moral lessons to the world. Like our prophets before us, we must continue to advocate of the essentiality of universal justice and moral values. Moral values, as Emile Durkheim suggests is far more essential and relevant to the well being of modern society than are religion and faith. Germany and all the countries that have persecuted Jews in the last two millennia did not lack religion nor were they without faith. What they lacked was a sense of justice and morals. Modern societies which are religiously and ethnically heterogeneous must place morals ahead of faith because faith by its very nature is discriminatory and divisive while morals are universal and integrative.

The memory of the Holocaust and all the tragedies that Jews have endured for the last two millennia should not lead us to the desire of revenge. The world has had enough wars and tragedies that were rooted in revenge. Instead of striking back and follow the dictum of "eye for an eye" we should learn to overcome the desires of revenge that is part of the primitive mentality of the Id. Instead of striking back we need to have the courage of uncovering the reasons of our hostilities even when such knowledge may be inconvenient and negating beliefs that we may hold sacred.

Remembering one's experiences and internalizing the experiences of others who suffered wrongs is central to our moral development. It is only through furthering morals that we may become humane humans. Social life without morality and the continual moral advancement is tantamount to the regression to a life governed by the base instincts of the Id. Without morality we can lead only an animal like existence. It is not technology that makes us human - but, morality for without it, as one of the Jewish prayers tells us, the pre-eminence of humankind over the beasts is naught.

Nations and communities, whether religious or secular, like individuals, are innately hedonistic. We seek pleasure and the absence of pain. Raking up memories, especially if such memories that include the pain and hurt and shame that are brought on by the experiences of great losses, must be critically examined both by the victims and the victimizers. To seek total forgetfulness and the avoidance of pain is deleterious to the growth of moral humanism. This is especially true with the Holocaust. No individual, nation, or religion should seek to advocate a motto "forgive and forget" We should, indeed, forgive if forgiveness is earned, but we should never forget. We must remember Amalek, Egypt and the Germans for the evils they committed. It is imperative for us to keep the memory of the Holocaust alive not because we wish to seek retribution, neither because we seek to indulge in self pity, nor because we seek self-glorification. Rather, we must keep the memory alive so that we may learn the pitfalls that critically unexamined human activities can lead to. It is only through remembering that we can eliminate the mistakes of the past Let us, therefore, remember and learn and let us light the candles in the memory of those who died in the dark days of fascism. More importantly, let the light of these candles illuminate the future path in which the world walks, a path governed by moral principles.

We must be careful not to trivialize nor to routinize the memorization of the Holocaust as we do with most of our instituted memorial days. For instance, the Fourth of July holiday, a day that was designed to commemorate the struggles of those who gave their lives and fortunes for achieving freedom and independence has been trivialized. Instead of remembering and contemplating how we must maintain our independence for which our ancestors have paid a heavy price, we use the day instead for pleasurable pursuits. Similarly, the Jewish commemorative

Faith and Conflict

day "tishah b'av" the ninth day of month Av, (usually occurring in July) a day that the ancient rabbis aside to remember and lament the destruction of the two Holy Temples in Jerusalem is now hardly observed in the present. As a member of the rapidly dwindling minority the "she'erith hapleyta" a member of the remnant of the Holocaust survivors I am very concerned that we will forget this event and more importantly forget the moral lessons that the world must learn from it. I hope that the annual the Yom Hashoah will maintain its significance and not become irrelevant, routinized and trivialized. If indeed we wish to solve the many problems that were the core reasons for historical injustices we must learn that first and foremost we must seek the implementation of justice and not worry about salvation. Salvation is assured only if we establish a world that reflects the ultimate moral value of justice and concern for the welfare of the whole world.